Advertising

Michael Pollard was born in Sussex and educated at London University. After spending ten years as a teacher, he entered educational journalism and has worked for numerous newspapers and journals both as a staff writer and as a freelance contributor.

Michael Pollard's many books include general and educational titles, and he has written guides on getting into, and working in, advertising.

SERIES EDITORS: Stephen Coote and Bryan Loughrey

Advertising

Michael Pollard

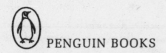 PENGUIN BOOKS

PENGUIN BOOKS

Published by the Penguin Group
27 Wrights Lane, London W8 5TZ, England
Viking Penguin Inc., 40 West 23rd Street, New York, New York 10010, USA
Penguin Books Australia Ltd, Ringwood, Victoria, Australia
Penguin Books Canada Ltd, 2801 John Street, Markham, Ontario, Canada L3R 1B4
Penguin Books (NZ) Ltd, 182–190 Wairau Road, Auckland 10, New Zealand

Penguin Books Ltd, Registered Offices: Harmondsworth, Middlesex, England

First published 1988

Filmset in Linotron 202 Melior

Typeset, printed and bound in Great Britain by
Hazell Watson & Viney Limited
Member of BPCC plc
Aylesbury Bucks

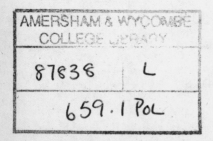

Contents

659.1 POL

Author's note

Many people in the advertising business have generously given their time to help me with this book on the understanding that, so that they could speak freely, their comments would not be attributable. I am most grateful to them, and have respected that condition.

I should also like to thank, in particular, the Advertising Association, the Advertising Standards Authority, the Association of Independent Radio Contractors, the British Direct Marketing Association, the Independent Broadcasting Authority and the Independent Television Companies Association for their help and co-operation. It should be made clear that any comments on their respective spheres of operation are my own.

Finally, the companies, agencies and publications named in my three case histories are entirely imaginary and have no connection with any similar existing or former organizations.

Michael Pollard

1 The advertising business

Advertising consists of messages, paid for by those who send them, intended to inform or influence people who receive them. At one end of the scale, a poultry-keeper who puts an 'EGGS FOR SALE' notice on his gate, or a market trader who directs a stream of hoarse inducements to passers-by, is advertising. So is the international company whose name is emblazoned on an airship.

It must be said that some people in advertising dislike such simple analogies. Perhaps they are affronted by the huckster image of the market trader. Perhaps they fear that if it is suggested that their work can be done by a poultry-keeper's lad with a paintbrush, someone may ask why advertising should be such a hideously expensive business, employing some of the cream of the nation's education system and surrounded by so much theory and mystique. The fact remains that the ad-man is blood brother to the showman, the market trader, and anyone else with something to sell. Advertising strays away from such simple truths at its peril. If it is not careful, it ends up producing, for example, television commercials which fail to name the product they are selling, or catch-phrases which stay in the mind but are not specifically related to their product. Advertising can easily get carried away with its own cleverness. And there have been enough abysmally unsuccessful advertising campaigns for those in the business to be over-confident. So let us, ducking if necessary the missiles from the advertising world, stay for the moment with the poultry-keeper.

How to sell eggs

This is more appropriate than it may seem at first sight, since over the years the skills of a large number of advertising people have been addressed to the problem of how to sell eggs. Eggs are, in some ways, difficult things to sell. The supply varies (and therefore so does the price) at different times of the year. Leaving aside personal prejudices between brown and white, farm fresh and free range, large and small, one egg is very much like another. The competition is not within a specific market for eggs but between eggs and other quick convenience foods, mostly high-volume processed foods which match eggs keenly in price. Added to all this, egg consumption in Britain has been in decline for some years; in 1972, the average Briton ate 4½ eggs a week, but by 1982 this had dropped to 3½. These facts do not greatly concern our lone poultry-keeper, but we will return to them later.

The man who puts up an 'EGGS FOR SALE' board at the gate may or may not sell his eggs. It may be simply that not enough people – or not enough potential egg buyers – pass by. The notice may not be prominent enough. The wording may be too small to be read from passing cars. Or there may be doubts about the product – the price may be too high, or the chicken-runs may look too scruffy.

The poultryman may well wonder whether his choice of words is at fault. Perhaps 'NEW-LAID EGGS' or 'FRESH EGGS' would be more effective. (But he must be careful, or he may fall foul of a trading standards officer – in the egg world, 'new-laid' and 'fresh' have precise meanings.) Perhaps he should have used red paint rather than black. Perhaps he could have thought of something more arresting – say, '**STOP! EGGS HERE!**'

For all its simplicity, this example brings out some of the aspects of advertising which concern large organizations as much as keepers of hens. For example:

* Reaching the market. Our man's market is not simply 'passers-by'. It is 'passers-by with an interest in buying eggs' – probably women driving to and fro on their school or station taxi-runs. If the market isn't there, the notice is a waste of time. *Is the medium right?*

* Suiting the message to the medium. A roadside notice should be bold enough to attract attention, but not so bold as to put passing motorists in the ditch. Our man's notice should be clearly visible from both directions so that, say, a woman sees it on her way

past with the children and is reminded to stop on the way back. *Is the message right?*

* Cost effectiveness. It might be worth while getting the notice painted by a professional signwriter. But this depends on the size of the market, the number of eggs available for sale, and the duration of the egg-selling season. *Is the budget right?*

* Judging the effect of the campaign. Easy enough, of course, for the egg-man. But, in any other circumstances, *how do we get feedback?*

* Media planning. Would more eggs be sold by a postcard in a shop window or a small ad in the local paper? *Is the planning right?*

All these have parallels in the real world of advertising:

* Reaching the market. For a long time, advertisers of eggs have reached their market through television and the more domestically orientated women's magazines. The decline of the cooked breakfast led to the promotion of 'going to work on an egg'. More recently, eggs were positioned in the health foods market by ads showing, for example, the jockey Willie Carson about to tuck into an egg salad.

* Suiting the message to the medium. Egg advertising is suited to television and to full-colour full-page spaces conveying a simple message. No one needs to be told what an egg is. The advertiser's trust is placed in simple, attractive images.

* Cost effectiveness. The media used for egg advertising are the most expensive. But the market is universal and the supply of product virtually endless. In any case, egg advertising is forced into the most expensive media because that is what the competition uses.

* Judging the effect of the campaign. Except in the case of a totally new product, this is difficult and absorbs a great deal of advertising and marketing effort. In view of the figures given earlier, it might be thought that the egg campaigns between 1972 and 1982 were not successful. However, without them, the decline in egg consumption might have been even sharper, given that eggs had to fight not only changing breakfast habits but also medical concern about fried foods and about the constituents of eggs themselves.

* Media planning. The selection of media and the timing of ads are skills vital to effective advertising. For example, egg production peaks in spring and early summer, when the market for shop eggs is also disturbed by farm gate sales. But at least egg production is reasonably predictable. For advertisers with products more vulnerable to sales fluctuation, such as beer, ice-cream and soft drinks (all at the mercy of summer weather), life is more difficult.

The advertising process

The source of an advertisement – the advertiser – might be an individual, a family business, a company, a pressure group, a nationalized industry, a multinational corporation, or a government department. In most cases advertising is processed through an agency. The means by which it is distributed is the media. Its intended destination – the market – may be all households where domestic washing is done (as with a detergent commercial on television) or a few hundred 'opinion-formers' (as in the case of an advertisement by a political pressure group).

The most visible face of advertising, for all of us, is the kind seen on television, in the popular press and on poster hoardings – the promotion of the brand names of consumer goods. This is the kind of advertising which attracts most attention both within and outside the business. It's where the big money is spent and where the big reputations are made. It also attracts most of the criticism of those opposed to advertising, a topic which is discussed in a later chapter. But it is often forgotten that there is a great deal of advertising that most of us never see. It appears in specialist business, professional and trade journals and is geared to highly specialized readerships. Advertising is about selling soap and cornflakes, but it is also about selling land drainage pipes to road contractors, extrusion machinery to plastics manufacturers, defence systems to overseas governments and industrial sand to makers of jam-jars. Although the budget of each individual advertiser may be minuscule compared with the big spenders in the consumer market, industrial advertising, as this field is known, grosses up to the second most important sector of the total advertising business, beaten only by the retail sector.

Table 1.1. *Advertising expenditure by product and advertiser groups, 1983*

Position	Advertiser group	£m spent
1	Retail	547
2	Industrial	388
3	Household and leisure products	382
4	Food products	313
5	Drink and tobacco	247
6	Savings and financial	222
7	Automotive products	185
8	Toiletries and medical products	157
9	Tourism, entertainment, foreign	136
10	Government	89
11	Nationalized industries	84
12	Publishing	52
13	Clothing	36
14	Charity and education	11

Source: The Advertising Association

Whether the advertiser is a large manufacturer wanting to sell a product to large numbers of people or a specialist with a product or service to sell in a small, closely confined market, the skills and techniques involved in the process are broadly similar. In either case, the match of product to medium, medium to message, and message to market is vital.

Advertising is all around you

There are people who claim that they are never influenced by advertising. They are all almost certainly wrong. In a developed society, you would have to live the life of a hermit to avoid being touched by advertising. The brand-naming of everyday products, the stylistic connotations of our choice of clothes or cars, furnishings or garden equipment, and the very ubiquity of advertising have made it part of our culture. It is no accident that children in the playground sing TV advertising jingles, or adaptations of them, alongside the more traditional playtime chants. At least one song – Coca-Cola's *I'd Like To Teach the World To Sing* – has made the transition from jingle to pop song, and hundreds of pop songs, to say nothing of more classical themes, have travelled in the opposite direction. The *Air* from the Suite No. 3 in D by Bach is known by that name to a relatively small number of people. As the theme of the Hamlet cigar ads on television, it is known to millions. Similar cross-fertilization takes place between television advertising and feature films, and between quality magazine advertisements and classical as well as popular art. From Toulouse-Lautrec to the film directors Alan Parker and Hugh Hudson, advertising has been the means of popularizing the highest techniques of the visual arts. At the same time, a few advertisers such as Benson & Hedges (in this case, it must be said, largely because of restrictions on what cigarette advertisements can actually say or even suggest) have achieved something approaching an art form of their own.

Just as the images of advertising influence the makers of the films we see, and its jingles seduce our children into re-forming the canon of playground songs, so its language – whether we like it or not – changes our perception and use of words. Certainly, advertising does some damage to language: 'new', for example, ceased many years ago to be a useful word, and 'fresh' is going the same way, while 'fragrance' (as in 'a new, fresh fragrance for that special date') has changed its meaning altogether. But much the same charge could be laid against popular journalism. At the same time, the language of advertising makes a contribution to our common culture. Echoes of the slogans of long-dead campaigns – 'Guinness is good for you', 'That's Shell, that was', 'Preparing to be a beautiful lady', 'Friday night's Amami night' – linger with all of us and are as much a part of the culture of this century as were, say, the street-cries of Victorian times. In conversation, an advertising allusion can be as apposite as – and to many people more comprehensible than – a literary one. Anyone who feels we fall too easily into the traps that advertising sets for us can take comfort from the failure of attempts to change the way we *pronounce* words, as in the long struggle, now thankfully abandoned, to persuade us via television to use a hard 'g' in 'margarine'.

Two other aspects of what might be called the cultural effects of advertising, especially TV advertising, might be mentioned here. One is that a large number of actors who specialize in commercials are known by face and voice, or both, to millions and yet remain anonymous. Few British viewers would recognize the name of John Hewer, for example – yet he has been playing Captain Birdseye of fish finger fame since 1967. The provenance of another familiar yet 'unknown' actor, Martin Fisk, will be revealed later in this chapter.

A second curiosity is that although, for years, toilet soap commercials have shown women washing their faces by dabbing lather directly on to the skin from their fingers, there is no evidence that this highly inconvenient way of washing has ever caught on, or that it was ever widely practised.

A visit to the doctor

In Western society, advertising is all-pervasive. Consider how it might enter into such a trivial occurrence as going to the doctor. As you go to the surgery, you pass outdoor advertising of various kinds: posters on roadside hoardings (consumer goods), bus shelters (public health campaigns), advertisements on the sides (more consumer goods) and backs (entertainments) of buses. On arrival, you leaf through a magazine or two in the waiting-room, and if your wait is a long one you are likely to pay more attention to the advertisements than you normally would.

Bored with magazines, you look around. You will find a number of advertising messages on the wall which may be for you. Some of these – announcing meetings of the Mother and Baby Club and so on – will be of purely local interest and derivation, but others take you into the advertising world proper, being posters produced for the Department of Health and Social Security, the Health Education Authority and other government or government-funded bodies. Have your children been vaccinated against whooping cough? Are you aware of the dangers of German measles to pregnant mothers? If you think you can drink and drive – don't. Isn't it time you gave up smoking? Why not become a blood donor? And so on.

It is your turn to see the doctor, and you go into the consulting-room. His calendar, his diary, his notepad and probably his ballpoint will have been provided by pharmaceutical companies so as to keep their names on his mind. (Strictly speaking, these items are, in advertising jargon, 'below the line' – indirect advertising – but they are advertisements none the less.) But the most direct influence of advertising on your outing to the doctor's comes when he writes out your prescription. Between them, the pharmaceutical companies spend millions of pounds each year on direct advertising to doctors in the medical press, and on various other forms of promotion ranging from conferences to ballpoint pens. You will probably never see any of this advertising, but it may well have a vital significance in your life.

Soap wars

All this activity, both direct and indirect and covering the whole range of media and the whole range of the population almost from the age when a child can interpret a simple message in pictures, is what makes up the advertising business. It commands the highest skills, as we have seen, of art, design, the use of language, film production, music and, in a word, communication. We may deplore the use of Bach to promote cigars, Dvořák to sell bread and, since 1984 when his music came into the public domain, Elgar to push almost anything; and some of the savageries committed on the English language by copywriters are enough to give grammarians apoplexy. But the skill – to some, a devilish skill – of the advertising people in pitching their messages to their markets can only be admired.

In the early days of advertising, it was enough merely to inform one's reader of the availability of a product, and of its qualities. A crude American soap ad from the early days is headed by two 'Before' and 'After' drawings. 'Before', we see a woman who looks as if she is in the critical phase of smallpox. 'After', her skin is clear. The copy underneath reads:

> Hood's Medicated Soap improves and beautifies the complexion. It is perfectly pure, wholesome, antiseptic, combines great healing, purifying and cleansing properties with the best elements for the toilet and the bath, and is the best skin soap in the world. All we ask for Hood's Medicated Soap is a trial, feeling confident it will so commend itself that hereafter you will use no other.

Many of the above claims, by the way, would not be permitted under today's stricter advertising codes.

But this kind of wordy appeal (still occasionally to be seen in ads for patent medicines) did not survive long in the soap industry. Soap was (and has remained) an ideal product for displaying the arts of advertising. It is an intensely personal product in daily use, associated with cleanliness, health and sexual attractiveness. In the nineteenth century, when branded soap first appeared, it was also associated more closely and urgently than it is today with the prevention of disease.

The soap industry provides one of the earliest examples of modern-style marketing, branding and advertising; and indeed Thomas J. Barratt, who was responsible for the early Pears Soap ads, was described by Northcliffe as 'the father of modern advertising'. Until about a century ago, soap was used fairly indiscriminately for all the purposes now covered by a whole range of products such as laundry detergents, washing-up liquids, scourers and household cleaners, as well as for personal use. The soap market was therefore a large and potentially profitable one. Two other factors had earlier helped to create conditions in which mass marketing could flourish. One was the building of the railway network, which made it possible for the first time to distribute cheap goods effectively and economically throughout the country. The other was the print explosion in the latter half of the nineteenth century, giving the manufacturer the opportunity to establish a direct link with the consumer, rather than relying on the wholesaler–retailer chain.

The advantages of this for the manufacturer were considerable:

> The wholesaler's stranglehold on trade was relaxed. Instead of dictating what the manufacturer should make, the wholesaler now had to respond to the demands created by advertising.

> A consistent or growing demand for his products enabled the manufacturer to achieve economies of scale by improved processes and machinery and the bulk buying of ingredients.

> A nationally established name provided a base for the
> introduction of new products.

It was against this background that A. & F. Pears Ltd hit upon the
idea of using well-known personalities such as Lillie Langtry to
endorse their 'famous English complexion soap', inaugurating a
genre, known as endorsement or testimonial advertising, which per-
sists (though, in Britain at least, under strict controls) to this day.
Later, for the family market, Pears acquired the rights in Millais'
'Bubbles' portrait. These were the first salvoes in a war that was to
dominate the British soap industry for several decades.

Sunlight Soap, the company founded by the first Lord Lever-
hulme, countered Pears with claims that its soap worked harder
for less effort – these were still the days of the washboard and the
scrubbing-brush – and, a powerful point when adulteration was a
common practice in the grocery trade, was superlatively pure. This
was backed up with a letter from an ex-president of the Royal College
of Surgeons, who 'employed the soap for his own toilet'. R. S. Hudson Ltd made a more wide-ranging claim for their soap: it was for
'washing, cleaning and scouring everything'.

The great soap advertising war of the 1890s and onwards serves to
illustrate another effect of marketing and advertising – the economic
one. To some extent, advertising is a war of attrition. Usually, the
battle sways to and fro between competitors, but occasionally one of
the contestants is mortally wounded: whatever happened to Strand
cigarettes, Motoring chocolate, Sky toothpaste? By 1914, the Lever
company (the lineal ancestor of Unilever) had absorbed both Pears'
and Hudson's together with a large selection of other British soap-
makers who could not afford to advertise so heavily. In the 1920s
Lever swept up many of the remainder. Interestingly enough, though
some brands like Hudson's have disappeared, others have been
retained and some even revived in recent years with 'nostalgic' packaging, showing that a brand name well established by advertising
has a commercial value stored away almost in folk memory.

Soap was the perfect product for the nursery slopes of modern
advertising techniques. It is, after all, much the same, give or take
its scenting ingredients: a mixture of fatty acids, potash, soda and
ammonia. It is cheap to make, non-perishable and easy to transport.

In marketing jargon, it is a low unit cost, high frequency of purchase item – something cheap which is bought often. What gives it its added commercial value, and therefore makes it worth promoting with vigour, is its branding and the loyalty – and the fight for loyalty – that that involves. All these remarks apply equally to the whole range of products, based mainly on detergents produced from petrochemicals, which have sprung from the original soap industry: fabric conditioners, shampoos, washing-up liquids, scourers, floor-cleaners, toothpastes and so on, all of which continue to command a large slice of the advertising spend. What observers of advertising may find curious is that, considering the long history of advertising in this field, the techniques actually employed are still among the least sophisticated: compare a detergent commercial with one for, say, breakfast cereals.

Does advertising work?

Everyone in the advertising business will want to answer with a rousing and unequivocal 'yes!' It would be wise to add a cautious 'usually' or 'sometimes'. The fact is that not nearly enough is known about how consumers behave, what influences their choice of products, or what makes a successful or unsuccessful advertisement. If there were a proven formula for tapping the interest of a consumer and making that interest last until it results in a purchase, life in the advertising business would be a lot easier, though it might well be duller. And if there were a *guaranteed* way of reaching the potential consumer, advertising would be more efficient. One study found, for example, that the owners of new cars were more likely to read and study advertisements about the model they had just bought than those about other models, the psychological justification for this being that they were seeking reassurance about their choice.

There are certainly some things that advertising, however much money and skill are put into it, cannot do. It cannot sell a product that is totally worthless. It cannot *create* markets; it can only identify them. It cannot persuade people to buy things that they do not want to buy, and people are more stubborn than many critics of advertising give them credit for. There is evidence for this in the fact that

80 per cent of all new food products launched in Britain fail. If advertising were infallible, this figure would be far lower if not nil.

One of the minor, but instructive, product failures of the 1960s in Britain was a washing-up cloth impregnated with detergent. As an idea, it had many appealing features: it was convenient; it was tidy; and it was two products for the price of one. One way of trying out a new product before the manufacturer commits himself to a national launch (with all the expense that that involves) is to test-market it in one or perhaps two independent television areas. The cloth was advertised on television in one area – and flopped disastrously. Housewives didn't see the point of it. They were well satisfied with the washing-up detergents available in plastic bottles (which were then still a relative novelty and a vast improvement on the powders previously used) and saw no need for change. What had seemed like a good idea had not been well enough researched before being brought to the market; and nothing that advertising could do could make up for that. (There was, however, an interesting sequel. The cloths, without the impregnation, later made a return to the market as the now familiar J-Cloths, and were hugely successful.)

Consumers may not only reject a product, however well advertised; they may misunderstand the message. For instance, it was discovered that a washing powder whose advertising was based on the efficacy with which it cut through dirt and stains was perceived as less 'kind to hands' than its competitors; while a TV commercial showing how an indigestion tablet 'dissolved stomach acid' was taken by many viewers to mean that the tablet should be taken in water.

By contrast, advertising can be so successful that it makes a huge impact on public taste and alters the structure of a whole industry.

The Yorkie story

Early in the 1970s, the confectionery firm Rowntree Mackintosh discovered a serious gap in its coverage of the market. Among chocolate blocks, its Aero was running a poor third to Cadbury's Dairy Milk and Mars's Galaxy, with less than 10 per cent of the chocolate-block market. After much research and testing of prototype chocolate blocks and brand names, Rowntree Mackintosh came up with Yorkie, a thick, chunky bar with a feeling of sustenance about it. (Traditionally, chocolate blocks are sold as nourishment, not as 'sweets'.)

The master-stroke of the launch of Yorkie in 1976 was the TV commercial, *Coast to Coast*, which was the work of the J. Walter Thompson agency. This ad – still well remembered even outside advertising circles although it was last used in 1979 – showed Yorkie helping a youngish, clean-cut truck-driver to get through his day. Yorkie gave him nourishment – but, as the Country-and-Western sound-track suggested, it was nourishment *with enjoyment*. By 1979 Yorkie was at fourth position among all confectionery lines, and by the next year it had raised Rowntree Mackintosh's share of the chocolate-block market to 30 per cent.

But Yorkie had done much more than that. It had altered the predilection of chocolate-buyers from the thin, rather brittle block they had been used to to the more challenging chunky style – a change that Mars and Cadbury's quickly recognized by bringing out their own chunky versions. Yorkie had also exposed just *how* thin and brittle, under the pressure of increased cocoa prices, the other blocks had become. But without its brilliant commercial (which, incidentally, made a star without a name of Martin Fisk, the actor who played the truck-driver) Yorkie might well, like so many other trail-blazing products, have withered and died. For Rowntree Mackintosh, advertising worked.

But advertising can only be successful in relation to the other elements in the whole production and marketing operation. However well the Yorkie *Coast to Coast* commercial may have stimulated demand, this would have done Rowntree Mackintosh no good unless the production of Yorkie had been set to meet that demand, the first supplies had been placed in position for the customers, and the confectionery trade made aware of the new product. The penetration of the UK car market by the Japanese in the early 1970s was made possible, at least partly, by the fact that British manufacturers could not deliver the cars they had advertised. It is doubtful whether any advertisement can be powerful enough to overcome the frustration of a willing customer who cannot easily buy the product.

The real thing?

The success or otherwise of advertising must also be assessed in terms of the advertiser's aims. There can be only one brand leader at any one time in any category of products. For the current brand leader, advertising may be aimed at keeping the product where it is in the league. Competitors in the same product area may not necessarily be wanting to reach number one; their advertising may be aimed at holding on to their present position. In practice, brand leaders are fairly impregnable unless a dramatic innovation, such as Yorkie, is made in a product area. Launching such an innovation into an established market can be likened to the take-off of an aircraft. It is a critical process with a point of no return and at least the possibility of disaster.

In 1985, in the United States, Coca-Cola pursued such an innovative course in an attempt to halt the slide of Coke against its archrival, Pepsi. In a single year, Coke's lead had fallen by almost 50 per cent, while Pepsi sales remained constant; given another year, Pepsi would have been inching ahead. People who buy cola are not buying merely a product but an image of themselves as consumers of that product, which is why image-building through advertising has always been crucial in the cola business. In the spring of 1985, Coke made what turned out to be a mistake: it introduced 'new formula' Coke, originally intended to replace the original formula. Since 'old' Coke had been advertised as 'the real thing', consumers were understandably confused. Within six weeks, the result of this confusion, as expressed at the checkouts, became too evident to be ignored, and old-style Coke came back on the market as 'Coca-Cola Classic', alongside the new product. Coke had hoped to administer a sharp electric shock to the US soft drinks industry but had managed (at considerable cost) only a small spasm, leaving the market in greater disarray than before and its advertising agencies burning much midnight oil.

Who is 'in advertising'?

When, in the later years of his life, Sir John Millais granted Pears the right to use his portrait of 'Bubbles' for advertising he was,

Table 1.2. *Division of IPA agency staff by function, September
        1984*

Function	%
Executives (directors, account executives and assistants and all other executives engaged on work requiring a knowledge of advertising not included in the specialist categories below)	23.5
Copywriters (scriptwriters and editorial)	5.7
Artists (including press and TV and film visualizers, typographers, photographers and exhibition and display designers)	12.5
Media (including press, TV, outdoor, cinema, radio and direct mail, and all staff employed in media planning, media research and buying)	9.3
Marketing services (including market research and copy research, merchandising, sales forecasting and analysis, economic intelligence and marketing campaign planning)	3.3
Public relations (including press relations and exhibition and product publicity)*	1.2
Mechanical production (including press and poster production, printing, traffic and art buying)	8.0
Audio-visual production (including TV, cinema, radio and film production)	2.6
Secretarial	13.1
Other (including accountancy and clerical work, telephone operators, receptionists and others engaged in work not requiring a specific knowledge of advertising or the specialized skills above)	20.8
	100.0

* Not all advertising agencies handle public relations, which is regarded as a separate discipline from advertising. The figure given in the table should be regarded as an indication of agency involvement in public relations, and not of the significance of public relations as a whole.

in a sense, taking the first step towards making advertising respectable. He was, after all, one of the leading figures in London's cultural life, a founder of the Pre-Raphaelite movement and a future President of the Royal Academy. In lending – or, rather, selling – his skills to the cause of advertising, he was to be followed by many creative artists, from Dorothy L. Sayers and John Piper to Leonard Rossiter and Orson Welles. But the images that advertising presents make up only one aspect of the business.

If someone told you that he or she was 'in advertising', you would (unless you were an insider yourself) almost automatically assume that it was in a creative role. It is the creative people – the art directors, artists, designers and copywriters – that we hear about; naturally enough, because if they are any good at advertising they will inevitably be good at advertising themselves; and, advertising being both volatile and highly competitive, this they need to do. But even in the agencies, where almost all the creative work is done, less than 20 per cent of the staff are engaged creatively. All the creative work done in all the agencies in membership of the Institute of Practitioners in Advertising is handled by fewer than 2500 people, and this includes people with supplementary functions, such as typographers and exhibition designers.

Advertisements have not only to be created. They have to be converted from ideas expressed in draft copy and artists' roughs ('visualizations' in the jargon) into finished work ready for the media. Space or time have to be booked for them, and the campaigns and marketing strategies into which they fit have to be planned overall. Research must be done on the appropriate media, and on the impact of the printed or broadcast advertisements. At the media end, advertisement managers have to provide potential advertisers and agencies with information about their readership or audiences. And between these elements – advertiser, agency and media – the traffic of the business has to be kept going. These are the jobs done by the other 80 per cent of agency staff, and by all those people who are in the advertising business but outside the agencies.

Art or science?

Advertising is sometimes compared with journalism or even (among some pretentious practitioners) with the arts, in that it seeks to influence, inform and sometimes even to entertain. But equally credibly it can be likened to the postal service. We, the consumers of messages, actually pay to read what journalists or poets or novelists have to tell us. When we open our mail, however, it is Aunt Nellie or the taxman or the bank that has paid to write to us. This is not the pedantic distinction it might seem; we are more likely to discriminate against messages that come to us uninvited. When they come, as advertising messages often do, in the middle of a television play or as a double-page interruption to an interesting article in a colour magazine, we may object very much indeed, and our instinct may be to shoot the messenger. Some people dread the postman's knock.

It is argued, with some justification though perhaps not as much as is often assumed, that consumers do in fact pay for advertising as a proportion of the cost of the products they buy; but this does not invalidate the postal analogy. We receive the messages about teabags and cornflakes, emulsion paint and cat food, whether we have 'paid' as consumers or not; and, by a strange paradox, if we have 'paid' by already buying the products, we have no need of the messages.

So, in one sense, the advertising business is a system for carrying messages; and in its early days, when agencies were merely responsible for placing advertisers' announcements with the appropriate media – 'posting' them, in other words – this was its sole function. However, as we have seen, it makes extensive and skilful use of the arts of writing, graphics, still photography, film and so on. It also leans heavily on science; and numeracy has become one of the qualities advertising people look for most closely in new recruits. As the cost of advertising increases, so does the importance of making sure that it gets to the maximum number of potential customers, and that its message has been received and understood. And behind this front-end statistical work lie all the statistics of marketing, which have to be collected, arranged and interpreted.

Advertising sometimes seems to be awash with statistics, of target audiences, circulations, readerships, costs per thousand, jolts per minute, Guaranteed Home Impressions, and so on. A cynic might suggest that advertising's apparent obsession with statistics masks a profound neurosis about what actually produces results. Such a neurosis might also explain the pseudo-scientific jargon used so heavily in advertising circles.

Attempts to apply scientific principles to advertising – to set up laws as immutable as Ohm's and Newton's – have, however, failed. It is tempting for advertising people, faced with the unpredictability and often the unverifiability of the effects of their work, to try to turn it into a discipline as reliable as, say, physics. But no sooner does anyone make a firm pronouncement on the subject than it seems that someone else conclusively disproves it. For example, one of advertising's gurus, David Ogilvy, once said that 'no one buys from a clown'

– in other words, that humour has no place in advertising. Countless campaigns have proved him wrong. Another one-time 'rule' of advertising was expressed in the couplet: 'Only in the gravest cases/Should you show your clients' faces'. The examples of Victor Kiam of Remington shavers (who was so impressed by the shavers, you may remember, that he decided to buy the company) and of the Norfolk meat processor, Bernard Matthews, and his US counterpart, Frank Perdue, have shot down this particular theory. It used to be taken as read that knocking copy (attacking the competition) was not only unprofessional but also counter-productive. You have only to look at a selection of current car ads to see how thoroughly this 'rule' has been thrown overboard. The truth is that, despite all the in-depth research and the scrutiny of findings, there is in advertising still a large element of hit-or-miss, more than most people in the business would admit. But then this is probably equally true of medicine, or the law, or teaching.

Case histories: 1

At various points in this book, advertising will be examined through three case histories, all of which are fictitious but based on real situations. In the first instalments below, the nature of the problems facing the three advertisers concerned are outlined and discussed.

Chase

Chase is a chocolate bar unknown to the trade; however, let us say that it was born in the mid-1930s. The idea then was that it would be the kind of chocolate a couple might share in the cinema, or perhaps out on a cycle ride in the country. It was seen as a wholesome product for wholesome young people, although its brand name had echoes of 'kiss-chase' and 'chasing the girls' (it was a sexist world in the 1930s). 'All right, then, Chase me' was the slogan that launched it and kept it afloat until the Second World War when, as with similar products, the market snapped up any chocolate it could get. Chase went on selling reasonably well through the 1950s, but then sales began to fall away, and the downward spiral grew increasingly steep with the launch, backed by heavy TV advertising, of new competitors. By the mid-1960s Chase, once a market leader, had dropped almost out of sight.

Chase is made by a large confectionery company with a range of other lines in the popular confectionery market. For a while management concentrated on the company's other, better-selling brands. But one or two of the management team went on worrying about Chase. Back in the 1930s it had been a winner, the company's flag-carrier. Now, there seemed to be three choices:

To kill off Chase and stick to the more successful lines.

To kill off Chase and replace it with a new chocolate bar.

To revive and re-launch Chase.

The first step was to decide what had gone wrong with Chase. Before venturing into a full-scale market survey, the marketing staff were asked to produce a preliminary report. There were three main points:

1. The competition. Chase had been overtaken by more aggressively promoted brands. Compared with these, the promotion of Chase was under-financed, and this in turn undermined confidence in the product in the retail trade.

2. The product was devised for the days of large cinema audiences, when going to the pictures was the favourite form of an evening out. Cinema admissions rose steadily during the 1930s and the Second World War, to reach a peak of over 1600 million in 1945. From that time, they nose-dived until 1982, when they bottomed out at 65 million, since when they have risen very slightly. Putting it another way, as many people went to the cinema *in a single fortnight* in 1945 as during the whole of 1982. Sales figures of Chase matched the graph of cinema admissions fairly closely.

3. The image. The successful 'All right, then, *Chase* me' campaign of the 1930s was still remembered and gave the product its current image. The contemporary equivalents of the cinema in young people's lives were the disco, the pub and perhaps the wine bar. Showing a girl a good time now meant more than taking her to the pictures and sharing a chocolate bar with her.

Researching the problem

In spite of all this, a re-launch of Chase remained, within the company, a desirable proposition:

If the company did not maintain a presence in the chocolate bar field, competitors might sense weakness and attack in other product areas.

The equipment existed to expand manufacture of a chocolate bar, and no large investment would be needed, at least initially.

Given the choice between a re-launch of Chase and the launch of an entirely new product, it was argued that a re-launch from a low base was preferable to a launch from zero, and would save development costs and time.

It was decided to research the feasibility of a re-launch. A market research programme was commissioned, with the aim of answering the following questions:

* What is the total market for chocolate bars, by age, sex and social group?
* What is the ranking of competitive products in the market?
* Who buys Chase now?
* Who used to buy Chase but now buys something else?
* Are Chase purchases occasional or regular?
* Why did people stop buying Chase?
* What do ex-Chase buyers buy now?
* What do people in general think of Chase?
* In which sectors of the market could Chase hope to expand?

The first two of these questions could be answered by consulting marketing statistics, of which there is an unceasing flow. For the rest, it was a matter of getting field workers out into the streets with their clipboards.

The questions would not, of course, be put in the bald form in which they appear above. For example, the question 'Who buys Chase now?' would be asked by showing a card on which a Chase wrapper was mounted and asking, 'Do you recognize this product?', followed by the supplementaries 'Have you ever bought one?' and 'How recently?' The results might be expressed in the eventual report like this:

Recognized	Bought	In last week	In last month	In last six months
28%	16%	3%	5%	8%

In a more detailed survey, these results would be shown broken down as between male and female respondents, and as between different age-groups and social groups. Similarly, the question 'What do people in general think of Chase?' would be put obliquely, perhaps by showing a number of drawings of different faces and asking respondents which they thought most likely to be Chase-buyers.

The survey revealed that Chase was well down in the chocolate bar ratings, with 4.6 per cent of the market. However, the brand was recognized by over a quarter of respondents, of whom just over half had bought a Chase bar fairly recently. What was wrong with Chase, the research suggested, was that it was old-fashioned. There was a suggestion that the chocolate tasted slightly soapy, the way cheap chocolate used to taste. But it is notoriously easier to collect negative responses than positive ones; in view of the 4.6 per cent market base, it was decided to go for a re-launch. The marketing department was asked to draw up a short-list of advertising agencies who would be invited to pitch for the business.

Taplow's Hardware

Robert Taplow's grandfather set up shop in Thrapsley High Street in the 1920s, selling paint, timber and small ironmongery. He reckoned it wouldn't be long before the owners of all the semi-detached houses going up round Thrapsley would need to start repairs and redecorations, and, stretched as they were by their mortgages, they'd have to do the work themselves.

Old man Taplow was right. By 1935 he had two other shops in neighbouring towns, and he was doing pretty well. But by the time Robert Taplow came into the business in 1970, things were looking less prosperous. The big DIY chains were beginning to emerge, offering a wider choice of goods, discounted prices and more room for display. Jim Taplow, Robert's father, toyed with the idea of selling out to one of the big groups, but a moment's second thought told him that none of them would be interested in his premises, with their small frontages, cramped back yards and no parking space.

So Taplow's muddled on, selling smaller cans of paint to people who had no cars to take them to the out-of-town DIY stores. Their market was the small spenders – people who thought in terms of 'a lick of paint' rather than redecorating the whole house; who had put up all the shelves they needed; who weren't going to go in for major works at their time of life; and who did not subscribe to the throwaway view of interior decoration, responsive to each shift in style.

One day Robert decided to make a tour of the rival stores to see what Taplow's were up against. He spent a week at it, making notes, listening to what the customers were saying to one another, imagining himself as a customer. By the end of the week, he had made a discovery.

Going to a big DIY store was all very well if you knew exactly what you wanted, and how much of it, and how to set about the job you proposed to do. But there was no one to advise you. It would be no good going up to the checkout and asking how many rolls of paper you needed for a bedroom twelve feet by ten. There was no one to tell you what paint to use on your outside oil-tank. The assistants were mere shelf-stackers who knew nothing about the merchandise and could only refer you to the instructions on a tin. And what was more, Robert concluded, these stores were not really *selling*. They were simply putting their stuff on display for customers to choose or not, as the case might be.

Taplow's staff, Robert knew, all had a wrinkle or two when it came to house decoration and maintenance. One or two of them had been in the building trade at one time; most kept their own houses immaculate. Taplow's might not be able to match the big stores' prices, but they had two things to offer that the stores didn't: (i) advice, and (ii) service. The stores, Robert had noticed, were not particularly interested in taking orders for goods not in stock. They would do so if pushed (and if anyone could be found with an order book), but grudgingly. And with goods ordered specially, the stores often lost their price advantage.

Taking up the challenge

Robert took these thoughts to his father and uncle, the other partners in the business. If they chose their own battleground, he urged them, Taplow's could fight back. They would, in effect, be selling not tools and cans of paint but advice and service.

Apart from taking space in the parish magazine to oblige the vicar, Taplow's had never advertised; they had seen no need to. Now, Robert suggested, was the time to see what advertising could do for them.

'It'll cost us,' warned Jim.

'I don't mean in the *Daily Express*, Dad,' said Robert. 'There's the *Thrapsley Guardian*, and the free paper that comes through the door every Thursday. And local radio. Why don't we at least find out how much it would cost?'

Beaver Generators

If you lived in a country house in the days before the advent of the public electricity supply, you were likely to have a Beaver Generator somewhere in the outbuildings. Beavers were sturdy, reliable and easily maintained by a handyman. Beaver Generators were established in 1900 and grew steadily until the 1930s, when, after a slight check as the result of a decline in the home market, a thriving export business was built up. This and government orders sustained the company during the war years, and there was a brief revival of business during the period of power-cuts in the early 1970s; but by 1980 Beaver were in serious difficulties.

A chance remark by the son of one of the directors, who was working in computers, brought about a change of direction. Computer installations, it seemed, were vulnerable to failures or fluctuations in power, and there was a need for standby sources of electricity. This seemed to be a field which Beaver, with its experience, could enter.

The kind of generator needed, it turned out, was more sophisticated than Beaver had been used to producing; but technical expertise was hired and, by 1982, the company had a prototype ready to launch on the market.

But a problem now appeared. Beaver was a name well known in

general engineering but not in the computer industry. The new generator would have to be marketed as an entirely new product to an unknown field. At this point, Beaver decided to call in a local firm of advertising and marketing consultants.

2 The broadcast media

The theory and practice of advertising have been developed and refined largely in the United States, but their influence has been pretty well universal. Elements of the American example can be seen even on the poster hoardings of Communist bloc countries. But when it comes to the use of the media, each country's standards and practice are its own, determined by a variety of factors which include geography, history and politics. A comparison between the broadcast media of the United States and of Britain shows how these influences fashion advertising's use of the media:

> Commercial radio was established in the United States in the 1920s but was not significant in Britain until 1973.

> The United States has thousands of local radio stations, many of them appealing to specialist audiences and competing for listeners in the same communities; whereas commercial radio coverage of Britain is on an exclusive-territory basis and is still not complete.

> Commercial TV in the United States had a ten-year lead on Britain's which began in 1955, and also benefited from experience of commercial radio operations.

> US television is based on competing local stations, some relaying networked programmes and others specializing in news, light entertainment and so on from local sources. British independent (commercial) TV is broadcast on two channels only, one (Channel 4) relaying a national programme (though commercials originate regionally) and the other (ITV) networking programmes nationally at peak hours.

> There is minimal government control of broadcasting in

the United States. In Britain, independent broadcasting in general, and its advertising in particular, is strictly controlled by the Independent Broadcasting Authority, and ultimately by the Home Office.

The absence of nationally circulated mass-market newspapers in the United States (which may disappear with the introduction of fax systems and other new technology) throws more emphasis than in Britain on broadcasting as a medium for national advertisers.

Cable TV has quickly established itself in the United States but has made only a slow start in Britain.

Other countries, too, have their quirks. France's list of items that must not be advertised on television seems, at least to non-Gallic eyes, to have been chosen at random. Austria prohibits television advertisements aimed at or featuring children. In Scandinavia there is no TV advertising at all.

Television advertising in Britain

In thirty years, starting from scratch, television has grown to be by far the dominant advertising medium in Britain in terms of the amount of money spent on it. In 1983 television advertising accounted for 40 per cent of total advertising expenditure, excluding classified; this despite the fact that television is, by common consent, an unsuitable medium for certain types of advertising and certain types of products, while other products – including such potential big spenders as cigarettes and certain medicines – may not be advertised on the TV screen.

The independent broadcasting system in the UK is a curiously British compromise between state control and limited but closely regulated free enterprise. The Independent Broadcasting Authority, the appointment of whose members is subject to Home Office approval, oversees the operation of commercial television and radio. It selects the programme-making companies by awarding franchises, fulfils a watchdog role over such matters as balance, taste and legality, controls advertising, and owns and runs the network of transmitters and communications between them (in some cases jointly with the BBC). The IBA itself is not a maker of programmes. The controls available to it include the banning of particular programmes or advertisements (though in practice, as is described in a later chapter, unsuitable advertisements almost always get weeded out before they reach the IBA), and its ultimate sanction is to refuse to renew, or even in extreme cases to call in, its franchise to a programme company. This last sanction has never been used, though at least two TV programme companies have skated perilously close to it. However, each round of franchise renewals features the disappearance of one or more companies which have failed in some way or other to meet IBA requirements.

The putting together of the schedules of the ITV network is in the hands of fifteen regional independent television companies, plus TV-am, which is a separate, nationwide operation. (There are actually fourteen ITV regions, but two companies share the franchise for the lucrative London area.) Some programmes are produced in the companies' own studios, while others are bought in from overseas (notably from the United States) or from independent British producers. Although, in peak viewing hours, all regions usually show the same programmes, each company detaches itself from the network for the commercial breaks and for continuity – the linking announcements and trailers between programmes. Advertising time in each region is bought and sold individually, although in fact all regions may sometimes show the same commercials at the same time. The occasional topical commercial is networked in the same way as programmes; but normally commercials are broadcast from film or tape supplied to the regional programme company and made up into batches of suitable length.

Channel Four's brief, when it was set up in 1982, was to provide an independent television service distinct in style and programming from the main ITV network. The output is controlled by Channel Four Television, and the schedules are national; there is no regional 'opting out', except for the commercial breaks. Channel Four schedules are made up from programmes made by the regional ITV companies or bought in from independent producers in Britain and overseas. Channel Four itself makes no programmes; its role is simi-

Table 2.1. *Regional ITV companies, headquarters, regional coverage and number of households*

Company	HQ	Region	House-holds (000s)
Anglia	Norwich	East Anglia	1449
Border	Carlisle	The borders of England and Scotland, and the Isle of Man	242
Central	Birmingham	East and West Midlands	3411
Channel	St Helier	Channel Islands	44
Grampian	Aberdeen	North and North-east Scotland	447
Granada	Manchester	North-west England	2554
HTV	Cardiff	Wales and part of South-west England	1907
London Weekend	London	Greater London, 7 p.m. Friday to Sunday closedown	4215
Scottish	Glasgow	Central Scotland	1278
TVS	Southampton	South of England	1910
TSW	Plymouth	Devon and Cornwall	611
Thames	London	Greater London, Monday to 7 p.m. Friday	4215
Tyne-Tees	Newcastle-upon-Tyne	North-east England	1328
Ulster	Belfast	Northern Ireland	460
Yorkshire	Leeds	Yorkshire, Humberside and Lincolnshire	2233

TV-am, from its headquarters in London, broadcasts breakfast-time independent television seven days a week, and sells its own advertising time.

lar to that of a book publisher. Its advertising time is sold by the regional companies, which fund the programmes from their receipts. Channel Four Television is responsible to the Independent Broadcasting Authority for the programmes and to the regional companies for the commercials. The object of this rather complex arrangement is to break down the direct relationship between the size of audiences and the quality of programmes, making it possible for Channel Four to screen items of minority interest. In Wales, Welsh-speakers are served by their own version of Channel Four, Sianel Pedwar Cymru (known as S4C), whose programmes come from HTV, BBC Wales and from independent producers.

One other company is involved in providing independent television programmes, though it has no connection with advertising.

This is Independent Television News (ITN), which is responsible for the national and international news service on both independent television channels, and is paid for on a fee basis by the regional companies.

The regional ITV companies are not all equal. The potential audience for the two London companies is over 95 times that for Channel Television. It naturally follows that the burden of programme-making for ITV falls on the regional companies in proportion to the size of their potential audiences. In practice, the companies break down into three groups:

> the 'big five': Thames, London Weekend, Granada, York-shire and Central

> the middle group: Scottish, Tyne-Tees, HTV, TVS and Anglia

> the small fry: Border, Channel, Grampian, TSW and Ulster

As can be observed by watching the credit logos of ITV programmes over a couple of days, the big five provide the majority of programmes, particularly the costly dramas and documentaries shown at peak times. The middle group produce a smaller number of net-worked programmes, but are fairly well represented. The small fry concentrate largely on output for their own areas. Each regional company is charged with the duty of providing some regional news and feature output, and all the mainland companies contribute staff and equipment for big national occasions, sports programmes and other outside broadcasts.

Television in the Irish Republic is, of course, outside the scope of the Independent Broadcasting Authority and is broadcast by Radio Telefis Eireann, responsible ultimately to the Irish government. There are two channels, both of which take commercials.

Advertising on TV

The rules about advertising on TV in Britain are laid down, and strictly overseen, by the Independent Broadcasting Authority. (The controls on the content of TV advertisements are described in a later chapter.) Here again, there is a contrast with the United States, where controls are much more relaxed on both the content and frequency of commercials. Close viewing of a television series bought in from the United States will show how often the action pauses to allow for a commercial break. It is also permitted, in the United States, for advertisers to sponsor whole programmes, filling them with virtually as many references as they like to their products.

In Britain, TV advertising time is sold on a 'spot' basis. A 'spot' for an individual commercial may be as short as seven seconds or as long as sixty seconds or, on fairly rare occasions, even longer. 'Spots' are grouped together in batches which appear between programmes and at intervals during them. In theory, commercials during programmes should come at a natural break, but in practice the natural break may be created merely by an announcement by, say, a quiz show presenter that 'We'll see you again after the break'. Natural breaks must, however, be clearly signalled, which is why they are always preceded and followed by a still caption card. (In the early days of ITV, optical effects such as a shooting star or a black and white 'wipe' were used between individual commercials to remind the viewer that he was watching advertisements, but this requirement has lapsed.) There must not be more than six minutes of commercials per hour, averaged across the hours of transmission, nor more than seven minutes in any one hour. This is in contrast with the practice in some European countries, where commercials are grouped in batches of up to twenty minutes.

The structure of independent television in Britain, with its combination of regional and spot facilities, favours advertisers with large budgets and proves disadvantageous to many smaller advertisers. On the national launch of a new product, a large national company can saturate the whole country's commercial breaks with repeated showings of the launch commercial. A regional launch can be promoted by choosing one or more ITV areas. But the smaller advertiser – say, a retailer with a catchment area round one of the larger cities – is less well catered for. In the first place, the sheer cost may be against him, with a single thirty-second peak-time spot in the London area priced at about £12,500 and even in the thinly populated Border TV area at well over £1,000. Secondly, the large ITV areas deliver audiences too large for many advertisers. For example, an advertiser of, say, fitted bedroom furniture in Norwich who buys time on Anglia TV will be paying for audiences as far away as Peter-borough, Luton and Milton Keynes whom he may not want and cannot service. There is a strong case to be made (and it would be technically possible) for access to TV advertising to be enhanced for the smaller advertiser by 'editionizing' some commercial breaks so that they are shown only in sub-areas of the TV regions.

The shape of the TV audience

For roughly four million people in Britain, the day begins with breakfast television, roughly divided half and half, during the week, between the BBC and ITV (BBC does not broadcast breakfast tele-vision at weekends). The weekday pattern continues, after breakfast television ends, at a low profile until midday, when it begins to climb to a lunchtime mini-peak round about 1 p.m. to 1.15 p.m. The audience slides slowly away again until, with the return of children from school and, in winter, the gathering dusk, the graph starts to climb towards 4 p.m. Shortly after 5 p.m. audiences gather steeply until, half an hour later, some 60 per cent of homes are viewing. There is a plateau until about 7 p.m., when more people gather round their TVs. The peak is reached at nine o'clock, after which the audience begins to steal away, fairly slowly until 10 p.m., but much more sharply after that.

This, of course, is the pattern of an ordinary, average sort of week-day. A blockbusting programme such as the 'Who shot JR?' episode of *Dallas* in 1980 or a national event such as the Derby would distort the graph, not only during the programme concerned but also in the time around it. What is perhaps surprising, however, is that the huge increase in unemployment in the late 1970s and early 1980s made very little difference to the pattern of weekday daytime viewing; and, despite occasional wishful newspaper stories about people get-ting tired of television and switching off in large numbers, both the pattern of viewing and the number of people actually viewing at any particular time remains remarkably constant. So does the appeal of television to specific age, sex and class sectors of the population. Children aged up to fifteen are heavy viewers, boys watching more TV than girls of the same age. Suddenly, in mid-teenage, the picture changes and these formerly insatiable audiences become the lightest viewers of all. Marriage and the arrival of children bring them steadily back to the box, and from then on television plays an increasingly important part in people's lives – though in women's more than in men's. For many elderly people, effectively isolated in their homes by illness, lack of transport and fear of going out, life almost literally revolves round TV. In terms of social class, the most affluent are the lightest viewers of TV and the least affluent the heaviest.

All this naturally influences the suitability of TV as an advertising medium for specific products or services. It explains why Rolls-Royce cars are not advertised, but Fords and Vauxhalls are. It accounts for the preponderance of domestically orientated commercials featuring happy families enjoying breakfast cereals, instant soup and ice-cream puddings. It is responsible to a large extent for the persistent stereotype of the typical family as one in which the man is the breadwinner, the woman stays at home all day using plenty of domestic appliances and consumer products, waiting for their 2.4 children to come home from school – a situation true of only one family in five. The infinitely caring and unharassed mother in the Fairy Liquid commercials is clearly not a single parent; nor, even, is the nervy mother taking Anadin for her headache.

How time is sold

The buying and selling of television airtime has become an increasingly sophisticated business. Although the TV companies talk of selling 'time', the trend in recent years has been away from selling particular slots towards selling audiences or, as advertising people say, selling 'demographics'. A time element is still involved, of course; no toy manufacturer wants his commercial to go out during the late film; and some advertising, such as that for national newspapers, necessarily demands evening viewing. It is still possible to buy time specifically in the middle of, say, *Coronation Street* – but the advertiser must expect to pay heavily for the privilege. The technique of selling audiences has been developed to ease the companies' difficulties caused by the six-minute limit. Despite the higher cost of peak-time (mid- to late-evening) spots, these are the most attractive to advertisers since they deliver the largest and, in terms of age, sex and class, least discriminative audiences. The natural result would be that the companies could easily fill their breaks during these hours up to the IBA limit, but would at other times be left with slots either partially empty or capable of being filled only at knock-down prices. By selling audiences gathered over a period in a selection of slots, the companies can offer a package consisting of peak and off-peak times. The basis of the offer is that the commercials will be seen, over a number of slots, by a guaranteed number of people; they will have, in the trade term, a certain number of Guaranteed Home Impressions. This leaves the company free to put together the commercials that make up each break as it likes, provided that the combination of slots reaches the advertiser's paid-for target. Detailed research enables the companies to identify not only the crude size of the audience but also its type, so that they can offer guaranteed impressions among, say, housewives under thirty-four, adults of a particular social status, and so on. Perhaps it should be explained at this point, since the word will recur frequently, that 'housewife' is, in the advertising business, not a sexist term but a technical one, signifying the person mainly responsible for looking after the home.

Although the ITV companies issue rate cards showing their prices for the various slots and packages on offer, a good deal of wheeling and dealing goes into the buying of television airtime. This is dictated by the fact that peak time, throughout the year, is in a seller's market whereas off-peak time is often in the buyer's. There are discounts for quantity, to local and first-time advertisers, and special rates for those who will accept whatever slots are available and give them up if someone comes along with a better offer. The need to abide by the IBA limits and, when programmes are being networked nationally, to make commercial breaks fit exactly into the time allotted for them, enforces flexibility in the scheduling of advertisements. Shrewd time-buyers can take advantage of this flexibility, and it is for this reason that the buying of time is best left to an advertising agency or a specialist media buyer.

Who's watching?

The whole structure of television advertising – the rate cards, the discounts, the Guaranteed Home Impressions and all the rest of it – rests upon accurate information about who watches television, and when.

The week ended Sunday, 3 November 1985, was, in TV terms, a fairly ordinary one. There was no major sporting event, no news crisis, no media happening like the Miss World show or the Eurovision Song Contest to distort viewing figures. Table 2.2 shows which were the top twenty audience-pulling programmes that week; as it happened, ten were shown on ITV and ten on BBC1, and this reflected roughly the total audience pulling-power of each of those channels. The day of transmission is also shown.

Table 2.2.   Top twenty TV programmes for week ended Sunday, 3 November 1985

Rank	Programme	Network	Day	Viewers (million
1.	EastEnders	BBC1	Thu/Sun	19.25
2.	EastEnders	BBC1	Tue/Sun	18.05
3.	Coronation Street	ITV	Mon	16.75
4.	Coronation Street	ITV	Wed	16.35
5.	Last of the Summer Wine	BBC1	Sun	15.70
6.	Full House	ITV	Wed	15.05
7.	Bergerac	BBC1	Fri	14.60
8.	'Allo 'Allo!	BBC1	Mon	14.55
9.	Just Good Friends	BBC1	Thu	13.45
10.	Crossroads	ITV	Wed	13.05
11.	Howards' Way	BBC1	Sun	12.70
12.	Crossroads	ITV	Tue	12.55
13.	Whicker's World	BBC1	Sun	12.50
14.	Emmerdale Farm	ITV	Tue	12.20
15.	Girls on Top	ITV	Wed	12.15
16.	Minder*	ITV	Wed	12.05
	Crossroads	ITV	Thu	12.05
	The A-Team	ITV	Sat	12.05
19.	Wogan	BBC1	Fri	11.80
20.	Blankety Blank	BBC1	Fri	11.70

* In this particular week, Minder was not shown in the London ITV area. The previous week, when the series was completely networked, it attracted 14.70 million viewers and was in eighth position.

For comparison, the top programme on BBC2 that week was an

instalment of Scott Fitzgerald's *Tender is the Night* (5.50 million, though this was made up of two audiences, one for the initial showing and another for the repeat in the same week). The top Channel Four show was the Monday instalment of the soap opera *Brookside*, at 6.25 million, though this too was a compilation of the audiences for the original showing and the Sunday repeat. It should be noted that the figures given in Table 2.2 for BBC1's *EastEnders* were similarly compiled from two showings.

Several things stand out straight away from a glance at Table 2.2. Of the twenty programmes, eight were broadcast at the weekend (counting Friday evening). All went out in peak time. No fewer than eight were half-hour episodes of soap operas. All the top twenty could be classified as light entertainment. Sixteen lasted no longer than half an hour, which perhaps suggests something about the powers of concentration of the mass audience.

A comparison of the table with the programme schedules for that week reveals something else. On Sunday evening, 15.70 million people tuned in to watch *Last of the Summer Wine*. All but three million of them stayed on for *Howards' Way* which followed, and almost all of this audience went on to see *Whicker's World* after that. On Friday, all but 100 000 of the *Wogan* chat show audience stayed to watch the following *Blankety Blank*, by coincidence a show originally hosted by Terry Wogan but which, by this time, he had handed over to Les Dawson. Similarly, ITV had a fairly loyal following on Wednesday night when only 1.30 million of the viewers who saw *Coronation Street* failed to stay tuned for *Full House*, and over 12 million went on to see *Girls on Top*.

The question of the loyalty of audiences ('inheritance', as it is known) is a hotly debated one among TV schedulers. It is, of course, of vital importance to the ITV companies in terms of revenue, and to the BBC in terms of status. It was certainly once true that whichever channel managed to capture a large audience early in the evening could look forward to holding on to most of it, unless it put on some spectacularly unappealing programme such as an arts magazine or a political discussion. This accounts for the placing of the soap operas early in the evening; the fact that when BBC1 launched *EastEnders* as its first venture into this type of programming for some years in 1985 it was positioned at 7 p.m. and later at 7.30, suggests that the

argument still holds some sway. But now that there are four channels
to choose from, which in many homes can be switched without
moving from one's armchair, plus the option of putting on a video –
to say nothing of the older alternatives such as going down to the
pub – channel loyalty looks less strong than it once did. Jeremy
Turnstall, in The Media in Britain, suggests that 'it seems to work
only over very short time spans; the audience may wait briefly to see
what the next offering is like, but having seen it, may quickly switch
away'. There are signs that schedulers, having once done their best
to build up regular viewing habits, are now trying to break them
down, at least among viewers of the rival networks – hence the
Tuesday–Wednesday–Thursday 'mini-series', which cuts across the
audience for weekly instalments 'on the other side'.

The top twenty table, for all its interest, is only the visible tip
of the iceberg of audience research. Its source is the Broadcasters'
Audience Research Board (BARB), a body jointly funded by the
ITV companies and the BBC and set up to bring some consistency
to audience information which, when each arm did its own research,
was often wildly conflicting. But BARB produces audience figures
not only for each programme on each channel throughout the day
(except for a few whose audiences are so sparse as to defy research
procedures) but also for each fifteen-minute segment of viewing
time. It is this detailed information, analysed, fed into computers
and processed by statisticians, which forms the basis of the ITV
companies' projections of their audiences for particular slots of airtime.

How do we know?

BARB's information comes from three distinct sources: from a sample of television sets fitted with meters which record the sets' on-
time and also which channel is being viewed; from a sample of
families who keep daily diaries of their viewing; and from surveys
which reveal individuals' 'appreciation' of the programmes. To the
outsider, all research of this type looks fairly suspect, an impression
that is not helped by the consistent failure of opinion polls to forecast
election results correctly; but the BARB system, tested over thirty

years by its predecessors and refined under BARB's own control, seems as accurate a tool as TV schedulers are ever likely to have.

Nevertheless it begs a number of questions, most of them concerned with the *penetration* of television advertising. Easy as it is to find out how many sets are switched to which channel at any given time, it is less easy to find out how much attention is being paid to them. In many homes, TV is used as a clock – the set is on most of the day, whether anyone is watching or not. In others, people may come and go while the set is on, catching perhaps only a few moments of a programme. When it comes to the commercial breaks themselves, the doubts grow even stronger. Many people take advantage of them to put the kettle on or see to the baby or put the cat out. (The switching-on of electrical appliances during the break in a big-audience nationally networked programme, such as the first TV showing of a notable film, causes significant fluctuations in the national power supply.) Even if the audience stay in their seats for the commercial break, they are likely to discuss the programme among themselves, count the stitches in their knitting, pick up the paper to see what's on next, or fit another piece into their jigsaw puzzle, taking no notice of the commercials; and these activities are beyond the reach of research.

New technology has, on the whole, been unhelpful to television advertisers. The remote-control switch has led to the phenomenon of 'zapping' – switching to another channel, often during the commercial break, to see what's on there. And VCRs, now owned by one-third of the homes in Britain, enable viewers watching programmes they have recorded earlier to 'zip' – fast-forward through the commercials and get on with the programme. Taken together, all these factors make something of a dent, if no more than that, in the credibility of published viewing figures as an index of the viewing of commercials. But it may be said in favour of the British ITV system, from the advertiser's point of view, that the relative brevity of commercial breaks encourages a viewer who is at all interested in a programme to stay with it. Also, the multiplicity of short breaks means that a commercial can be repeated several times during a day's viewing, either in full or, as often happens, in a shorter (and of course cheaper) 'reminder' format. The criterion used in television advertising is not that the target audience will have seen every showing of a commercial but that it will have seen at least one in any one batch or 'burst'.

Summing up, it can be said that the ideal product or service for television advertising is one that is (i) national, (ii) in the mass market, and (iii) capable of being demonstrated or explained simply. Of course, many items that do not come into these categories are advertised successfully on television; but the further they stray away from these criteria, the more difficult successful use of TV becomes.

The very nature of television imposes some obvious restrictions on its use for advertising. It is best at conveying short, memorable, punchy messages, and cannot be used at all for giving detailed information. Beyond this, the IBA imposes more complex restrictions than are suffered by any other medium. As was noted earlier, the structure and cost of independent television disadvantage the smaller and more local advertisers.

Non-network TV

The facilities for advertising provided by the regional ITV companies on the ITV network and Channel Four are likely to remain the most important aspect of television advertising. But other recent developments will become increasingly significant over the next few years. Even so, with its thirty-year lead and its ability to deliver large audiences about which detailed research is available, ITV as we know it will continue to be the dominant force. It has to be added, too, that all three of the developments mentioned below have been beset with either teething troubles or a poor response from their potential audiences.

Teletext, also known as *videotex*, is broadcast throughout the UK by the ITV network under the name Oracle (Ceefax is the BBC equivalent). It provides printed information on screen, and can also show graphics and fairly crude illustrations. Teletext can be received only on sets fitted with a special de-coder, which has inhibited the take-up of the facility by the general public. However, it does offer advertisers something they are denied by ordinary TV commercials – the ability to present detailed information; and, as it is the viewer who decides when to look at another 'page' or to switch off, it is highly suitable for showing comparative information or details which have to be copied down. It has obvious attractions for such advertisers as travel agents, airlines, coach services and mail order firms. Both Oracle and Ceefax provide, as a subsidiary service, sub-titles for selected network programmes for the benefit of the hard of hearing.

Cable TV, using optical fibre cables, has built up a substantial following in the United States but has had a rather slower start in Britain. One difficulty is that cable systems depend on subscriptions and Britain is not a society geared – in the mass market, at any rate – to the subscription system. This is the reverse of the situation in the United States, where the population is used to buying magazines on a subscription basis and one TV channel, the Public Service Network, depends on subscription income. Since, if there is a TV set in the house, British families have to pay for a TV licence to support the BBC whether they watch BBC programmes or not, and ITV comes, as they see it, 'free', the difficulties of the cable subscription sales staff may be imagined. It remains to be seen whether this resistance can be overcome, but at the time of writing the omens do not seem to be good.

Satellite television is used in the United States in conjunction with cable, a combination enforced by geography. The proposal in Europe is for DBS – Direct Broadcasting by Satellite – for which viewers will have to erect dish aerials, either individually or on a district basis. The system will have an obvious appeal for multinational advertisers, who will be able to reach markets such as Scandinavia where the national TV networks do not carry advertising and many other European countries where advertising is strictly limited. In Britain, early optimism about DBS was confounded by subsequent bickering between the BBC and the IBA, which had planned a joint initiative. After this uncertain beginning, in 1985 the IBA announced that it was going ahead with preparations for a British satellite system which could provide up to five additional channels. Radio Luxembourg, traditionally a pioneer in radio and television because of its favoured position within range of a number of different cultures and languages, has announced that it will join in a DBS system for western Europe. What remains to be seen is whether the public's thirst for television is insatiable, and whether the advertising market can stand so much division and sub-division of the media.

Independent local radio

Commercial radio is a relative newcomer to the British media scene, having been introduced in 1973 in London and spreading fairly slowly across the country since. Many areas do not yet have coverage, but more stations are planned. Financially, independent radio companies have had mixed fortunes, and most of those outside the large conurbations are always fairly close to, and sometimes below, the borders of profitability.

Independent local radio is controlled by the Independent Broadcasting Authority, which issues franchises to local radio companies for specific areas, much as it does for the ITV companies. There has been talk of a national independent radio network to compete with the BBC, but no firm plans have been announced and, if it comes, it is still many years away.

There is a limited amount of co-operation between independent local radio stations, but there is no networking of programmes on the scale practised by ITV. However, all take the national and international news service of Independent Radio News.

ILR stations are allowed to include up to nine minutes of advertising per hour. Reflecting the prevailing British belief that television is potentially dangerous but radio fairly harmless (it is no accident that radio broadcasting of Parliament was introduced with relatively little fuss, while TV broadcasting has found dramatically less support), the IBA's controls on radio commercials are less stringent than those on television, and are largely delegated to the radio companies. Much of the advertising is local, and this is sold by the stations themselves. National advertising is handled by centralized sales agencies, but radio is used by national advertisers almost exclusively to support advertising in other media. The medium is not strong enough on its own to justify the cost of heavy use for the national market, and, as is noted later, there are practical difficulties. However, local radio offers smaller advertisers a genuinely local medium and to some extent fills in the gap created, as mentioned earlier, by the structure and cost of ITV. A particularly useful feature of ILR is that it reaches the 15–24 age-group, who are the lightest viewers of television.

Poor relation?

There has been a good deal of criticism, from both within and outside the advertising business, of the quality of advertisements on local radio. In a report on a survey it conducted in 1983 into reactions to independent radio, the London ILR station Capital Radio admitted that 'Radio commercials are the poor relations of television commercials in terms of production values and entertainment. Radio attracts more criticism for poor presentation and repetition rather than variation and correspondingly appears to achieve lower brand recall than television.' Translated, this means that listeners tend to switch off, mentally if not literally. This may be due to the fact that in order to achieve target audiences commercials have to be repeated far more often on radio than on TV, and therefore cracks in presentation, feeble humour and other irritations tend to be more evident. But undoubtedly radio advertising in Britain suffers from its relative youth and from the lack of a body of experience in its use. In the United States, where commercial radio has been operating for over sixty years, the quality of radio commercials is far higher and there is no difficulty in persuading top entertainment names to take part in them, or top copywriting talent to write them. By contrast, few copywriters for British radio seem to have got very far beyond the idea that anyone can sell anything if they speak in a funny voice. No doubt, also, the advertising content of local radio reflects the poor quality of much of the programming. Excepting a handful of large city stations such as Capital and LBC in London, Piccadilly in Manchester and BRMB in Birmingham, local radio runs largely on a mixture of not-quite-pop records, chat shows, phone-ins, and sadly understaffed news bulletins. One local station, to save the expense of sending a reporter by taxi to a large fire about five miles away, sent him down to the car-park (to get an 'outside acoustic') to broadcast an 'eye-witness' account from there. It is not surprising that advertisers and their copywriters take their cues from such a cheap programme policy. Nor is it surprising that so many ILR stations are in such financial difficulty.

Radio time is sold on a spot basis like TV time, with the cost related to the size of audience at any particular time. ILR's listening pattern reflects the general picture of the use made of radio in Britain, the

graph of ILR listening following the BBC radio line almost exactly.
The peak period is in morning 'drive time', from about 7 a.m. to 9 a.m.
peaking at about eight o'clock, and the attention paid by ILR stations
to traffic conditions reflects this. The audience then tails away, with a
slight lunchtime revival, until it picks up again for the drive home.
There is another slighter peak at about 11 p.m., when people are going
to bed or coming home from an evening out, but by midnight ILR has
a total audience of perhaps half a million and falling.

Luxembourg and others

Radio Luxembourg is the only survivor of a handful of commercial
stations based on the Continent which began beaming broadcasts to
the UK in the 1930s. Capitalizing on the dull fare provided by the
BBC on Sundays, these stations built up substantial family audiences. They were responsible for the first jingle – We Are the
Ovaltinies – to enter British folk consciousness. Since it restarted
broadcasting in English after the Second World War, Luxembourg
has concentrated on the teens-and-twenties market, employing
record shows virtually exclusively. Broadcasts in English begin at
7 p.m. and go on into the night. Luxembourg has a London office. It
is perfectly legal for British advertisers to use it.

This is not true of pirate radio stations. Under the Marine Broadcasting Act, it is an offence to advertise on, supply, or in any other
way support, offshore radio stations operating in international
waters. Radio Caroline and its various more temporary rivals cannot
therefore be regarded as potential media.

Radio Eireann's two radio programmes can be heard down the
western side of Britain, roughly from Glasgow to Bristol, but their
advertising is geared to the audience in the Irish Republic.

The next likely development in commercial radio in the UK is the
legalization of the, at present, 'pirate' community radio stations.
How this will develop as an advertising medium – almost certainly
suitable only for the local or highly specialist advertiser – remains
to be seen.

3 The newspaper industry

Because of the historical restrictions on broadcast advertising in the UK, newspapers held a dominant position in the British advertising business which went unchallenged, except by wartime newsprint restrictions, until the advent of commercial television in 1955. Since then, they have had to fight hard to hold on to a diminishing slice of advertising revenue which by 1983 had slipped to 24 per cent of total advertising expenditure, divided between the nationals (14 per cent) and the regionals and locals (10 per cent). In the 1960s, the casualties of this decline included the *Daily Sketch* and the *News Chronicle*, while the *Daily Herald* was transformed, in two painful stages, into the present *Sun*. Among Sunday papers, the *Empire News*, *Sunday Graphic* and *Sunday Dispatch* disappeared. Other areas of newspaper production were similarly affected, so that cities which used to sustain two evening papers were reduced to one, and the *Standard* became the sole survivor of London's three evenings for a period of some years.

The relative decline in the commercial power of the press can be gauged from the fact that in 1984 the *Daily Mail* was selling fewer copies daily than it had sold, in a far more crowded field, in 1928. More recent fluctuations indicate a very disturbed and uncertain market; in 1984–5 the *Mirror*'s circulation fell by 11 per cent, the *Daily Telegraph*'s by over 13 per cent – though the *Guardian* put on 15 per cent and *The Times* 27 per cent (from, of course, very much smaller bases). Changes in circulation either way mean problems for newspapers: falling sales show up at once in the cash flow and make it difficult to sustain advertising rates, but higher circulations mean increases in newsprint and distribution costs which have to be met before advertising rates can be put up.

National newspapers

National newspapers, as a group, are second only to television in attracting advertisement revenue, though they take less than half as much. The British stable of national papers, a Victorian tradition created after the spread of the railways, is a unique phenomenon; the daily press in other countries is regionally or even city-based.

Since 1985 the national newspaper industry has faced an upheaval bigger than any in its history. It has at last, long after its contemporaries abroad and even in the UK provinces, taken on board the 'new' technology (some of which, incidentally, is well over twenty years old): electronic typesetting, photographic platemaking and web-off-set printing. Old-style managements have been trying for years to move their printing out of the nineteenth-century, 'hot metal' era – each line of type cast in lead alloy, and each page cast again in the foundry – but until recently with little success. Suddenly – the industrial politics need not concern us here – the whole antiquated pack of cards has collapsed. Fleet Street itself has ceased to be a synonym for newspaper publishing as, one by one, the papers move out to new sites, mainly to the east of London. The long-standing distribution network based on the railways will increasingly give way to road-based carriers working from facsimile printing plants in key provincial locations. Already some newspapers, such as the Independent, launched in 1986, are produced and distributed in this way. All the national newspaper groups have announced similar plans, which are at various stages of implementation

The impact of these changes will be considerable. Web-offset printing from lithographic plates will enable the papers to offer, as many already can, full colour as a matter of routine, for both editorial and advertising. Until fairly recently, the national newspapers have had only two ways of offering colour. One was by 'pre-print' – colour pages printed in advance by web-offset and re-reeled so that they go through the press a second time to come out with the paper's other pages. The other was in their colour magazines, produced separately and well in advance of publication day. The main interest in colour as far as newspapers are concerned is, of course, in removing one of the undoubted advertising advantages of television. Food and clothing are two product areas from which they can expect to benefit. Against this it has to be admitted that, in the field of print, newspapers are up against stiff competition from magazines, particularly women's magazines, which have more leisurely schedules and are able to offer quality colour. By comparison, newspaper colour tends to look fuzzy, and it is not, at the present state of web-offset art, capable of reliable high definition.

There is another aspect to the new production pattern which could be important to advertisers in the future. Regional facsimile printing, as innovated by the *Independent* and likely to be copied ultimately by most national newspapers, offers the possibility of regional advertising similar to that of independent television contractors. Given the heavy involvement of newspaper groups in independent television companies, it would be surprising if this linkage did not lead to a new kind of advertising package whereby regions could be picked out for cross-media coverage including 'editionized' national newspaper advertising.

Meanwhile, the positioning in the market of the newcomers to the national newspaper scene remains a matter of conjecture. *Today*, launched in 1986, made an attack on the *Daily Express/Daily Mail* sector. The *Independent*, in the same year, shouldered its way into the quality market. Robert Maxwell's *London Daily News*, billed as a twenty-four-hour newspaper, was launched shakily in 1987 but soon collapsed without finding its market. There are rumours of other contenders for a slice of the market. How long these, and the various Sunday innovations, can survive depends largely on the purses of the backers; the ownership of newspapers has a powerful effect on the rich. The only certainty is that when the fall-out of the changes brought about by the new technology and the breaking of the print unions has settled down, the picture of the UK national newspaper industry will be very different from that of, say, the 1960s. But certain ground rules will be unchanged.

One of these is that quality newspapers can survive with far smaller circulations than popular ones. In 1960 the *News Chronicle*, a paper just on the popular side of the divide, folded with a circulation of 1 million, a figure that would send the management of *The Times*, the *Guardian* or the *Independent* dizzy with delight. The reason is simple: popular newspapers in Britain obtain between two-thirds and three-quarters of their revenue from sales and the remainder from advertising, whereas for quality papers the split is roughly reversed. These proportions have not changed significantly for decades. While popular papers are the favoured medium for advertising 'cheap goods bought often' – you would be unlikely to see an advertisement for margarine, for example, in *The Times* – the qualities can deliver the relevant up-market readership for, say, expensive cars, investments and 'opinion-forming' ads. The qualities also reach people who are relatively light, or extremely selective, television viewers, and they carry prodigious quantities of classified advertising – initially for jobs, but now extended to houses and quality cars – which the populars generally don't. They benefit too from City advertisements which, in the event of a share issue, can account for several full pages.

In fact, the distinction between 'qualities' and 'populars' is not quite as clear-cut as it might appear from their editorial content. In terms of their circulation among the social classes, the papers in the *Mail* and *Express* stable occupy a middle position and, for certain advertisers, can claim to be as influential in upper- and middle-class homes as the quality papers. (I am using these convenient class terms here as a kind of shorthand; but the advertising business and the media use a system of 'social grades' which is described in a later chapter.)

Broadly speaking, newspapers come in two sizes, broadsheet (like *The Times*) and tabloid (like the *Mirror*). This influences their use for advertising, if only for the obvious reason that a full page in a broadsheet paper looks to be of more significance than a full page in a tabloid. All the popular dailies, and all except the *Sunday Express* among the popular Sundays, are now tabloid. All the quality papers, daily and Sunday, have retained the broadsheet format and seem likely to continue to do so.

There are two figures related to newspapers which are of interest to advertisers: one is circulation, the other is readership. Readership figures are produced at six-monthly intervals by the National Readership Survey. The 15 million daily papers bought each day are read by some 44 million people, though 'read' is rather loosely defined as 'having read or looked at recently'. While the raw readership figure of a particular paper may not mean very much, the breakdown of sex, age and social class is a helpful indicator for advertisers as to its usefulness to them.

It should be noted that the term 'national newspapers' is not strictly accurate. The *Mirror*'s place in Scotland is taken by its stable-mate, the *Daily Record*. The three national quality dailies circulate lightly in Scotland, their place being taken by Scotland's own quality dailies, as noted later in this chapter. In many other parts of Britain it is difficult to obtain the quality dailies as a casual purchase. Sunday papers, both quality and popular, are more evenly and generously distributed.

Regional dailies

There are about twenty regional morning, and about eighty regional evening, papers in the UK. In addition, there are six regional Sundays.

Table 3.1.   *Towns and cities where regional morning papers are published*

Place	Title
Aberdeen	Press and Journal
Belfast	Irish News
	News Letter
Birmingham	Birmingham Post
Bristol	Western Daily Press
Cardiff	Western Mail
Darlington	Northern Echo
Dundee	Courier and Advertiser
Edinburgh	The Scotsman
Glasgow	Daily Record
	Glasgow Herald
Ipswich	East Anglian Daily Times
Leamington	Leamington and District Morning News
Leeds	Yorkshire Post
Liverpool	Daily Post
Newcastle-upon-Tyne	The Journal
Norwich	Eastern Daily Press
Plymouth	Western Morning News

Table 3.2. *Towns and cities where regional evening papers are published*

Place	Title
Aberdeen	*Evening Express*
Barrow-in-Furness	*North Western Evening Mail*
Basildon	*Evening Echo*
Bath	*Bath and West Evening Chronicle*
Belfast	*Belfast Telegraph*
Birmingham	*Evening Mail*
Blackburn	*Lancashire Evening Telegraph*
Blackpool	*West Lancashire Evening Gazette*
Bolton	*Bolton Evening News*
Bournemouth	*Evening Echo*
Bradford	*Telegraph and Argus*
Brighton	*Evening Argus*
Bristol	*Evening Post*
Burnley	*Evening Star*
Burton-upon-Trent	*Burton Mail*
Cambridge	*Cambridge Evening News*
Cardiff	*South Wales Echo*
Carlisle	*Evening News and Star*
Chatham	*Kent Evening Post*
Cheltenham	*Gloucestershire Echo*
Colchester	*Evening Gazette*
Coventry	*Evening Telegraph*
Darlington	*Evening Despatch*
Derby	*Evening Telegraph*
Doncaster	*Evening Post*
Dundee	*Evening Telegraph and Post*
Edinburgh	*Evening News*
Exeter	*Express and Echo*
Glasgow	*Evening Times*
Gloucester	*The Citizen*
Greenock	*Greenock Telegraph*
Grimsby	*Evening Telegraph*
Guernsey	*Evening Press and Star*
Halifax	*Evening Courier*
Hartlepool	*The Mail*
Huddersfield	*Huddersfield Daily Examiner*
Hull	*The Daily Mail*
Ipswich	*Evening Star*
Jersey	*Evening Post*
Kettering	*Northamptonshire Evening Telegraph*
Leeds	*Yorkshire Evening Post*
Leicester	*Leicester Mercury*
Lincoln	*Lincolnshire Echo*
Liverpool	*Liverpool Echo*
Manchester	*Manchester Evening News*
Middlesbrough	*Evening Gazette*
Newcastle-upon-Tyne	*Evening Chronicle*
Newport	*South Wales Argus*
Northampton	*Chronicle and Echo*

Norwich	*Eastern Evening News*
Nottingham	*Nottingham Evening Post*
Nuneaton	*Evening Tribune*
Oldham	*Evening Chronicle*
Oswestry	*Evening Leader*
Oxford	*Oxford Mail*
Paisley	*Paisley Daily Express*
Peterborough	*Peterborough Evening Telegraph*
Plymouth	*Western Evening Herald*
Portsmouth	*The News*
Preston	*Lancashire Evening Post*
Reading	*Evening Post*
Scarborough	*Scarborough Evening News*
Scunthorpe	*Evening Telegraph*
Sheffield	*The Star*
Southampton	*Southern Evening Echo*
South Shields	*Shields Gazette and Shipping Telegraph*
Stoke-on-Trent	*Evening Sentinel*
Sunderland	*Echo*
Swansea	*South Wales Evening Post*
Swindon	*Evening Advertiser*
Telford	*Shropshire Star*
Torquay	*Herald Express*
West Bromwich	*Sandwell Evening Mail*
Weymouth	*Dorset Evening Echo*
Wigan	*Evening Post and Chronicle*
Wolverhampton	*Express and Star*
Worcester	*Evening News*
York	*Yorkshire Evening Press*

Table 3.3.   *Towns and cities where regional Sunday papers are published*

Place	Title
Belfast	Sunday News
Birmingham	Sunday Mercury
Glasgow	Sunday Mail
	Sunday Post
Newcastle-upon-Tyne	Sunday Sun
Plymouth	Sunday Independent

As a group, the regional dailies are the third largest receivers of advertisement income, most of it regional in origin. A handful of the mornings and about half of the evenings are owned by one of the large provincial newspaper groups such as Thomson Regional Newspapers or Westminster Press. Of the remainder, some are owned by smaller regional groups such as Southern Newspapers

(*Southampton Evening Echo, Bournemouth Evening Echo, Dorset Evening Echo*) and a few (for example, the *Western Daily Press* and the *Bristol Evening Post*, published by Bristol United Press) are completely independent.

Managements of regional papers often feel, with some justification, that they are ignored by many national advertisers and their agencies. It has to be said that the conflicting schedules, formats and standard space sizes of the different papers cause headaches and additional work to media buyers trying to include them, though modern technology enables artwork to be optically expanded or compressed to fit any given space. The Regional Newspaper Advertising Bureau attempts to solve some of the practical problems, and to push the cause of regional newspaper advertising in general, but the fact remains that to plan a national or even a part-national campaign involving regional papers is a daunting prospect. The situation is not helped by the fact that in England (Wales and Scotland are rather easier in this respect) there is no correlation between the circulation areas of regional papers and the boundaries of the ITV regions, which makes combined regional paper and TV campaigns difficult to manage.

A further problem is posed by the diversity of the provincial mornings. These vary enormously in quality, standards and influence. The best of them, like the *Yorkshire Post*, are papers with a strong tradition, well respected and influential among regional opinion-formers as well as the general public. In Scotland, the *Glasgow Herald* and the Edinburgh-based *Scotsman* serve as their country's quality newspapers, and their existence accounts for the relative insignificance of the London quality dailies north of the border. At the bottom of the heap, there are one or two regional mornings – it would be invidious to name them, though they deserve it – which are little more than 'local rags', thrown together by ringing round the police stations and the Women's Institutes, with a nominal injection of national and world news provided by the press agencies. These include one of the biggest regional morning sellers. Nevertheless, whatever their standards or their circulations, the regional mornings tend to be thoroughly read. Together, they sell just over a million copies daily, excluding the *Daily Record* which, with its circulation of about 750 000, is in effect the Scottish edition of the *Mirror*.

The regional evenings – sharing sales of over 6 million daily – are a more homogeneous group, though they vary hugely in circulation from less than 20 000 to more than 300 000. They tend to be predominantly local in character and interests. Readership and appreciation surveys show that they are well liked by the public. People trust them (and therefore, by extension, their advertisers) more than the national press, and they play a far more significant part in decisions on what to buy and where to buy it. Many of them have Saturday football editions in season, sometimes printed on coloured newsprint for the newsagents' convenience, and so are dubbed 'The Pink 'Un' or whatever.

Much of the commercial strength of the regional dailies lies in their command of classified advertising. Taken as a group with the local weeklies, they derive about 57 per cent of their advertising revenue from this source, compared with about 17 per cent for the national papers. 'Classified advertising' has come to include much more than the traditional 'sales and wants'. It also takes in employment, property and – a significant element in most regional and local papers – used-car advertisements, many of which, although technically regarded as 'classified', appear in display or semi-display format.

Local weeklies

Local weeklies (a handful of which are in fact published twice weekly) are the most threatened sector of the newspaper industry. The main threat comes from free newspapers or 'freesheets', the local papers delivered weekly door to door, which have creamed off a great deal of advertising. Local weeklies are heavily dependent on advertisements, in the proportion of 85 per cent advertising to 15 per cent sales revenue.

Freesheets, which are discussed in more detail below, have been growing steadily in number since the early 1970s, and there are now over 600 of them, rapidly approaching the number of paid-for-weeklies. But freesheet competition is not the only problem. Another is that many of the local weeklies have had to face the cost of replacing equipment which had simply worn out. These papers, although now well printed on up-to-date equipment which is light on manpower, have to carry the inevitable interest burden of capital investment which in many cases was decided upon before the freesheet threat emerged.

The number of paid-for weeklies declined by a quarter, to about 880, in the years 1980 to 1985, and few months go by without news of further closures. The decline should not be over-dramatized, however. The disappearances were of 'titles', many of which were merely editions of each other with the bulk of the pages in common and local 'edition pages' inserted. Furthermore, some titles reorganized themselves into the freesheet category. Those that remain have wide acceptance and a thorough readership, and are particularly valuable in enabling the smaller advertiser to target his message precisely. However, a question mark must remain over the long-term future of many local weeklies. As they try desperately to compete with the freesheets by cutting costs, giving local reporters wider territories to cover, or by filling their pages with 'advertisement features' with little reader interest, they come to resemble the competition more and more closely.

If the local weeklies do go under, they will leave a very considerable hole in the media available to the small to medium business advertiser, especially to one with localized sales, and to national retail chains, which use them heavily to promote local stores. Those papers organized in a series of editions offer a flexibility not available elsewhere. The *Norwich Mercury* series, for example, has seven titles covering the shopping catchment area of Norwich. A Norwich trader could usefully take space on one of the pages that the seven titles have in common. A trader in one of the smaller Norfolk market-towns could advertise more economically on one of the local-edition pages. It is true that this facility is available with some freesheets published in series, but there is less reassurance about how well freesheets are read.

Freesheets

Freesheets draw their advertising almost entirely from local sources and generally from small businesses. Some make a serious effort to balance advertisements with editorial (though few are sufficiently well staffed to do so effectively), while others hardly bother with editorial at all, except perhaps for puffs for regular advertisers.

Freesheets are almost universally despised by the rest of the newspaper world, partly because they are often staffed and printed by non-union and untrained labour. Their distribution arrangements, using teenagers, are often shaky, and there is no real index to the depth or quality of their readership. Some of this animus rubs off on the advertising world.

The free newspapers are delivered – or, rather, they are supposed to be delivered – to every address in their circulation area. Their very lack of discrimination, though in theory offering blanket coverage, makes them suspect as advertising media, as many copies will end up in empty property, homes where nothing is ever read, houses occupied by people with little or no purchasing power, and so on. One or two in central London are got up in glossy magazine style; but freesheets generally are ill printed, badly laid out, unappealing to the reader and editorially lamentable. Their advertisements suffer from being packed cheek-by-jowl with others. In the absence of any convincing research, there must be some doubt about how closely, if at all, they are read, and they make little or no effort to establish a long-term following among either readers or advertisers.

Newspaper advertising

The most notable feature that newspapers offer their advertisers is flexibility of a kind not available in the other media. It is literally possible to decide today to take space in a daily news-paper tomorrow, and to do so, though this is not to say that life is thereby made any easier for newspaper advertisement departments. Because newspapers appear at such frequent intervals, they are equally suitable for the short, sharp campaign as for a longer, more sustained one. The multiplicity of titles enables the advertiser to pinpoint his market with great accuracy and relatively little wastage. Finally, the variety of spaces available – including, for some adver-tisers, the classified columns – caters for everything from a modest announcement of opening hours to a full-page blockbuster.

Against this must be set the generally poor print quality of news-papers and the absence, in general, of colour. Almost every day one can see examples of advertisements which, though they will have looked fine when proofed by a studio on art paper, have simply not stood up to the high speed and absorbent paper of news printing. Nor is there much hope that things will improve with the introduction of new technology. Provincial newspapers which have gone over to web-offset litho printing reveal a new set of problems: photographs, though reproduced to a smaller screen, tend to lose definition and become all-over grey, while there are considerable difficulties in achieving even inking when presses are run at high speeds. Web-offset litho introduces the availability of full colour – but in practice this often registers badly; that is, the colour layers do not lie exactly one on top of the other, giving blurred outlines and occasionally pictures that are completely unreadable. The 'spot colour' facility also available in litho – splashes of a second colour to relieve the black – can sometimes be useful and attractive, but all too often merely vulgarizes an already uninspired piece of artwork. Full colour and spot colour, of course, attract extra costs – considerably extra in the case of full colour.

Contrary to what is assumed by the uninitiated, advertisements are not simply stuck on to the pages of a newspaper wherever they happen to fit, except possibly in freesheets and on some of the more primitive local weeklies. Examination of a few days' run of a paper will show that there are certain spaces which are available for advertising, and others that are equally definitely not. (This applies to Britain. In the United States, one gets the impression that virtually any space is available, and this accounts for the formlessness and ill-design of American papers to British eyes.) For example, the leader page of *The Times*, and the main feature page facing it, do not, at the time of writing, carry advertisements (and indeed have never done so). The grounds for this are presumably that the very heart of the newspaper must not be corrupted by commercial considerations. Other papers take the opposite view. Assuming that the leader page merits particularly close attention, they charge a premium for advertisements that appear there and that therefore, by suggestion, have the particular approval of the management. Since leader pages are often also the letters pages – invariably among the best-read features of any paper – there is possibly sound commercial sense in the policy of allowing limited advertising there and charging extra for it. But this is only one example of the complex rationale that makes up any newspaper's scale of charges, known in the trade as its 'rate card'.

The cost of space

The basic unit by which advertisement space is bought and sold is the single column centimetre (s.c.c.). Single column centimetres are piled up and stacked side by side to make up various fixed spaces – 15 centimetres by 2 columns, for example, or 20 centimetres by 3 columns – which are offered on the newspaper's rate card; though in practice papers are prepared to sell many other areas of space, such as a strip running across the bottom of a page or a full column down the side, subject to negotiation. Some papers, though a declining number, also offer, at a special rate, their 'ears' or title corners – the spaces on each side of the title on the front and sometimes the back page; though these must surely be among the least attractive advertising spots on the market. There are normally special rates for full and half pages.

Rate cards tend to be individualistic, reflecting partly the tradition of the newspaper and its area, partly the prejudices of advertisers, partly the editorial make-up of the paper, and partly the whims of the proprietors. All this makes the buying of press space a highly complex business in which the merits of different spaces have to be weighed carefully against their widely differing costs.

The *Eastern Daily Press*, for example, is the regional morning paper for Norfolk, published in Norwich. It has, as a matter of fact, the highest circulation among the provincial morning papers in England, with over 90 000 copies daily. Discounting such categories of advertisements as births, marriages and deaths, classified, and employment, and looking only at display space, this leading provincial newspaper has no fewer than ten different rates per single column centimetre according to the position occupied by the advertisement. If you wanted to buy its front page solus spot, 20 centimetres by 2 columns, which is to say that yours would have been the only ad on the page apart from the two 'ears', it would have cost you, in 1983, £241.50. The same space semi-solus (one of two) facing the leader page would have cost you £176.50. If you were prepared to accept 'run of paper' (which means that your ad would go in wherever there was an appropriate space) you could have bought the same area of newsprint for £160.00. There was a range of other special positions like the front page solus – semi-solus leader, for example – and apart from the special positions quoted on the rate card at special rates, any position could be guaranteed for the basic 'run of paper' rate plus 25 per cent. This was to accommodate advertisers who wanted, say, a guaranteed right-hand page (a preference which, without much justification, still rules in some quarters) or a guaranteed position on the financial or books page or whatever. In addition, certain types of advertisements – company meetings, prospectuses and money issues, for example, in the case of the *Eastern Daily Press* – sometimes attract premium rates, while some newspapers have specially discounted rates for book publishers. (This is not because of any particular affection for books among newspaper proprietors, but because publishers tend to place their advertisements direct, without the intervention of an agency and therefore of agency commission.) Regular advertisers, especially if they occupy the same space on a regular basis, are often given series discounts. This sometimes leads to advertisers occupying traditional positions; for example, Harrods have taken the front page solus spot in the *Sunday Times* for many years.

The prices given on a newspaper's rate card are for the space *only*. Just as in radio or television advertising, production costs are extra. Any work that is necessary to produce the advertisement itself, such as typesetting and the making of blocks or artwork, is charged separately, except in the case of simple classified advertisements. In practice, most advertisements in all but local weeklies and freesheets arrive from outside ready-made, but local newspapers maintain their own art departments to produce advertisers' artwork and will typeset copy in their own composing-rooms.

Readership and the advertiser

The circulation figures of a newspaper – for all that those of all reputable papers are checked and verified by the independent Audit Bureau of Circulations which publishes revised figures twice a year – are only a crude guide to the papers' effectiveness as advertising media. The quality national newspapers are able to survive on their smaller circulations because of the buying power, either as individuals or by virtue of the positions they hold, that their readers have. To put it at its simplest, the manufacturer of a £25 000 car would be unlikely to advertise it in the *Mirror* because few of that paper's readers would be in a position to buy one. *The Times*, however, would deliver a large number of potential buyers. Conversely, a national supermarket chain that took 5p off all its prices would hardly choose the *Financial Times* to announce the fact; the *Mirror* would be an ideal place for that. Reinforcing a point made earlier (and this is what currently gives these papers a secure corner of the market), neither ad would be out of place in papers from the *Mail* or *Express* stable. The control of budget decisions likely to be in the hands of quality newspaper readers gives those papers an edge in advertising capital items and company services.

This brings us to the matter of readership, where there are two questions to be asked:

> How many readers does each copy of the paper, on average, have?
>
> What kind of people are they?

Obviously, readership cannot be verified as accurately as circulation but, by using a variety of techniques, readership figures are produced for some newspapers by the independent National Readership Survey and for others by surveys commissioned by the owners. 'Readership' in this context means 'read or looked at recently'.

Popular newspapers aim to be read by all the family; the qualities, by more specific groups of people. Where the quality dailies may lose out on family readership (the commuter takes *The Times* on the train and leaves the *Daily Mail* behind for his wife), they often gain on group readership. Many copies, notably of *The Times* and the *Financial Times*, are circulated in offices to be read, or at least glanced at, by six or more big spenders. Thus, at a time when *The Times* was selling 381 075 copies daily, it had, according to the National Readership Survey, 1 303 000 readers – 3.4 readers to every copy. In the same period the *Daily Express*, with 1 988 339 copies sold each day, had 2.4 readers per copy. The quality Sundays lack the group advantage of their daily counterparts, but they do have another. Arriving on a day when concentrated reading is often impossible or undesirable, they have a long after-life, and on commuter trains you can see people working their way through the business sections or the colour magazines well into the following week.

What kind of people are these readers? What sex are they? How old are they? What social class do they belong to? These are the basic questions to which newspaper owners want to find answers, in order to emphasize the suitability of their papers for specific kinds of advertisement. But sometimes it is necessary to go further; a paper planning an assault on a particular sector of the advertising market might carry out a survey to find out, for example, how many of its readers were interested in high-quality audio equipment, expensive cameras, sports goods, or whatever. A provincial morning paper like the *Eastern Daily Press*, say, or the *Yorkshire Post* might want to know how many of its readers were farmers or, putting it another way, what percentage of farmers were regular readers. The information gathered in this way goes to make up the newspaper's 'readership profile' which, if conscientiously and efficiently assembled, can be a valuable tool to the advertiser and the media buyer.

Newspaper advertising in practice

Analysis of the advertising content of different newspapers, which can be done by anyone with a few minutes to spare each day, is instructive in revealing their different characters and their varying advertising profiles. On an autumn day in 1985, the advertisements in national dailies at the extremes of the market, *The Times* and the *Mirror*, were examined closely. On that day, *The Times* consisted of 32 broadsheet pages, but three of these were a 'Special Report'. As *Times* 'Special Reports' are in effect advertisement supplements, with editorial support for the advertising, these were discounted; the figures in Table 3.4 are based on the remaining 29 pages. The *Mirror* consisted of 32 tabloid pages, which was at that time, mechanically, the *Mirror*'s maximum possible size. The number of column centimetres in the papers as a whole (excluding *The Times* 'Special Report') was almost exactly the same, as was the proportion (just over one-third) given to advertisements. The significant differences are in the products and services advertised.

Table 3.4.   *Advertisement space in typical issues of* The Times
and the Mirror, *by product or service category*

Category	The Times (s.c.c.)	Mirror (s.c.c.)
Charity	156	6
Auction houses	63	–
Workforce inducements	160	–
Banks, savings, investments	905	237
Business computers/office equipment	810	–
Health care	10	162
Loans	40	340
Corporate advertising	440	–
Theatres (outside classified)	68	–
Education (outside classified)	50	48
Business sites	7	–
Mail order	–	25
Household	–	55
Photoprocessing	–	25
Car leasing	–	100
Government (buying council house)	–	96
Government (Army Cadet Force officer)	–	96
Car insurance	–	195
Commercial vehicles	–	195
Car purchase	–	195
Cigarettes	–	195
Whisky	–	100
Automobile Association (motor-cyclist membership)	–	40
Classified	1952*	107

* The figure for classified has been adjusted to take account of the fact that *The Times*
ran nine columns of classified to the page, compared with eight on other pages and eight
on all pages of the *Mirror*.

Statistics can prove anything, but they can also reveal one or two
things. We can see that *Mirror* readers are expected to be:

> more concerned about health care
>
> more likely to be council house tenants
>
> more interested in borrowing money than in lending it
>
> less inclined than *Times* readers to be in a buying position
> in business
>
> less inclined to give to charity.

Possibly not many surprises here. In case it should be thought that
the last comment above is less than charitable, it should be pointed
out that the charity advertisements in *The Times* were asking for

postal donations and bequests, whereas the charitable instincts of
Mirror readers could be expected to be assuaged by street and door-
to-door collections. A slight surprise, indicating perhaps that the
identities of newspapers are not quite so clear-cut as might be
assumed, is the full page in the Mirror advertising car leasing, and
another advertising commercial vehicles. Eight of The Times's
advertisers, compared with thirteen of the Mirror's, included coupons in their ads.

The heavy use of both papers by savings, investment, loan and
insurance advertisers is significant. Such advertisers have a lot of
detailed information to get across, much of it obligatory by law. They
have to give examples of how the reader's money (or alternatively
his indebtedness, in the case of loan companies) will grow. Almost
all ads in these categories include coupons, the others giving freefone numbers. All were, in other words, geared in one way or
another to immediate response. Press advertising, in particular in
newspapers, offers three advantages to these categories of advertiser:
(i) immediacy, (ii) space for detail, and (iii) direct response. It is to
be hoped that anyone planning to save, invest or borrow money
would do so only after careful thought; but, paradoxically, the same
advantages of newspaper advertising apply to the impulse purchase
of, say, sets of cutlery, knock-down furniture and mail order
clothing. These are areas of advertising where newspapers (and their
colour supplements) have remained supreme and which they have
assiduously built up, since they saw other categories such as food
and domestic-appliance advertising largely swallowed up by television. For similar reasons, retail store groups' advertisements play
a large part in sustaining regional and local newspapers, where
detailed and up-to-the-minute price lists can be displayed.

A word about 'specials'

Virtually all newspapers try to stimulate their advertising revenue
from time to time by publishing 'specials', which may be called
'Special Reports', 'Special Features', 'Advertisement Features' or
'Advertisement Supplements'. These terms mean subtly different
things. In general, the editorial content of Special Reports and
Special Features is written by newspaper staff or commissioned

contributors, whereas in Advertisement Features or Supplements it is often supplied by the advertisers or a trade organization. The difference may be hardly discernible to the outsider, and in any case in advertising terms it is probably not significant.

'Specials' should not be confused with regular feature pages given to books, travel, women's interests and so on. The function of a 'special' is to attract additional advertising, and the editorial content is usually only a device to keep the advertisements apart. A quality newspaper's 'Special Report' on some obscure Middle Eastern state may have a long article on the front written by a public relations man but signed by the president, but this does not make it editorially any more valid than a piece by the chairman of the chamber of trade in a local weekly's 'Come Shopping' feature. Other typical subjects range from holidays and overseas business sectors (in the national papers) to Christmas Shopping in the High Street and Gift Ideas for Mother's Day (in the regionals and locals). Space in these 'specials' is often sold at different rates from those on the standard rate card.

In the days when the quality papers used to run their 'specials' as separate pull-outs in the middle, the floors of commuter trains were littered with discarded and unwanted paper. Now wiser, papers usually run 'specials' in with the rest of the pages so that they are not so easily ditched. But this does not necessarily give them any more credibility or readership and, perhaps with one exception, they are best avoided by advertisers who want value for money.

The exception concerns cases where an advertiser's absence may be noticed. If you are one of four building contractors with major contracts in that obscure Middle Eastern state and the only one not to take space in a 'special' about that country, it could look bad in public relations terms.

But in general, 'specials' are defective in principle. The basis of advertising is that the advertiser buys space or time because he has something to say; to buy simply because a newspaper has provided space in which to say something is a reversal of this, and something to be avoided.

4 Periodicals

A publication that appears weekly, fortnightly, monthly or quarterly (unless it is a local weekly newspaper) is known in publishing as a 'periodical'. For advertising purposes, this term can also be taken to cover the Sunday papers' colour supplements, since they have most of the characteristics, including a long 'readership life', of colour magazines carrying a cover price.

Something like 2000 periodicals of various kinds are published in Britain. They range from magazines like *Radio Times* and *TV Times*, with circulations of over 3 million each week and an appeal which cuts across regional, social grade, age and sex differences, to the bellringers' weekly *Ringing World*, whose circulation of just over 5000 is by no means the smallest. The number of periodicals fluctuates continually: established titles amalgamate or fold, while new social trends or crazes feed on and are fed by new magazines. For example, the growth of the home computer market in the early 1980s spawned a dozen or so magazines on the subject, so hopelessly dividing the advertising spend between them that only a handful survived more than a few issues. Jogging, aerobics, hang-gliding and snooker are other social fads which have created (generally short-lived) periodicals.

Clearly, it is difficult to generalize about a category of publications that ranges from *Woman's Weekly* to *Fur and Feather*, and so it is useful to break down this field into sub-sections.

Consumer magazines

Consumer magazines make up one large group. These are the kind of magazines most prominently displayed in the newsagent's. They include the two TV programme magazines, the weekly and monthly magazines for women and teenage girls, and those for men.

Radio Times and *TV Times* are the flagships of this group of media, and the envy of the rest of the periodical world. They seem to have all the advantages:

> Huge national coverage.

> They are 'editionized', so that they can deliver an advertiser's message nationally or regionally.

> *TV Times* editions match precisely, and *Radio Times* editions closely, the ITV areas, and can therefore be used in conjunction with television commercials without 'wastage'.

> They appeal to both sexes and across virtually the entire range of age and social class.

> They have an active life in the household for seven days, on which a copy will typically be consulted several times by everyone in the family who can read.

Small wonder that advertisement rates for these magazines, especially on the programme pages, compare with the highest in Fleet Street or on television itself. They have the bonus, too, that they are consulted at times when people are most likely to be relaxed and inclined to think about leisure and luxury; hence the high proportion of travel and mail order advertising. The phenomenon of television viewing guides is not confined to Britain; in the United States, the circulation of *TV Guide*, at over 17 million, is beaten only (and only just) by *Reader's Digest*. In Britain, the BBC and the Independent Television companies have held on to their captive readership by retaining the copyright of programme details and strictly controlling the amount of such information that newspapers may carry.

The markets for other magazines are more closely defined, though the larger circulations are among women's magazines. The three top-selling women's weeklies, *Woman*, *Woman's Own* and *Woman's Weekly* – all published by the same group, IPC Magazines – each have circulations around 1.25 million and readerships of four or more times that figure. Beyond these, aimed at the mass market of women, women's magazines start to break down into sectional or special-interest appeal. There is little in common between, for example, readers of *Cosmopolitan* and those of *True Romances*. They will not wear the same clothes, use the same scent, or even, if they smoke, smoke the same cigarettes. Readers of *Cosmopolitan*, unlike those of *True Romances*, will not be attracted by advertisements for cheap mail order clothes paid for in instalments; nor will *True Romances* fans provide a useful readership for manufacturers of fifty-guinea silk scarves. These are, of course, extremes; but the newcomer to the world of women's magazines may well be surprised at the extent to which this market has been broken down in terms of marital status, age, life-style and even sexual orientation. If nothing else, it proves (if proof were needed) that women are the great purchasers in our society, and that each sector of this vast purchasing power is worth fighting for.

Other magazines in the consumer group cover such specialized interests as cooking (*Home and Freezer Digest*), home-making (*Homes and Gardens, Ideal Home*) and diet (*Slimming and Nutrition*). Two curiosities among consumer magazines deserve a special mention. These are *Family Circle* and *Living*, which circulate largely through supermarket checkouts rather than the news trade. They cover general women's interests, with an emphasis on the housewife rather than the career woman. A useful feature for advertisers is that they can be 'editionized' for particular supermarket chains, so that they can be used to support in-store product promotions or special offers in specific groups of stores.

Notably absent from the UK publishing scene are general-interest consumer magazines in the *Time/Stern/Paris-Match* mould. The British general magazine of the *Picture Post* type folded with the coming of commercial television, largely because management did not react in time or with sufficient vigour to the television threat. Subsequent attempts to revive the genre – most recently Sir James Goldsmith's *Now!* – have been spectacular flops. The apparent absence in the UK of a market which, in the United States, sustains a 4.5 million weekly circulation for *Time* and over 3 million for *Newsweek* – and proportionately heavier circulations in some West European countries – is a source of some mystery, but there are two possible explanations. One is the emphasis in America on subscription sales. The British traditionally dislike forking out large sums of money in advance – hence the constant bickering about the cost of television licences – but contrarily expect to see copies of magazines on the news-stands awaiting casual purchasers. Only the women's weeklies, with their large circulations, can afford the huge amount of wastage – magazines being circulated in the news trade on a 'sale or return' basis – involved in this kind of purchasing pattern with a mere week's shelf-life. Monthly magazines have four weeks in which to attract the casual buyer – but, of course, they cannot be topical except in a general and well-prepared way. The second reason for this hole in the UK magazine market may be the fact that, alone among countries of its size, Britain's leading newspapers are truly national and therefore give good coverage at their different levels of the kinds of national issues that are the *forte* of the news weeklies. To take a random sample, the thalidomide scandal, the Anthony Blunt story, and almost all Royal Family coverage are items that would have been, and in some cases were, classic news weekly material abroad but which were covered *in extenso* in the UK national papers.

In Britain the Sunday colour magazines can be regarded as the legitimate, if lightweight, successors to the general-interest weeklies. The first colour supplements were launched when television was still in black and white only, and they could offer the bonus of colour. They have survived, with the addition of several new titles, since TV went into colour, largely by exploiting areas of advertising denied to TV by its very nature; for example, detailed and descriptive mail order offers, and ads featuring technical data about hi-fi, video equipment and cameras. The high proportion of coupon ads is noticeable and must pose problems for advertisement managers trying to avoid placing them back-to-back. The other notable feature of Sunday colour magazine advertisements is the number of ads for cigarettes and spirits, two product categories which are banned by the Independent Broadcasting Authority from the commercial television channels.

The proportion of advertising to editorial in these magazines is high: in typical 1985 issues, 55 per cent advertising in the *Observer Magazine* and 61 per cent in its *Sunday Times* competitor. The Sunday supplements make a strong feature of 'theme' issues, built typically round holidays, winter sports, cars and so on; but in contrast to some newspaper 'specials' it is characteristic that the editorial standards of these are generally high, using named writers. The advertising potential of these magazines is increased by the facility some of them offer for binding in catalogues, usually from middle and upmarket chain stores such as Habitat and Boots.

From time to time the supplements have made efforts to break through the restrictions imposed by the long printing schedule of photogravure and to print relatively newsy material; but for all this, they are a long way from being news magazines in the *Time* sense, while their editorial content generally remains trivial when compared with the main newspapers of which they are a part.

There is no question but that magazines for women dominate the consumer periodical field. Though it is often said glibly that there is no equivalent batch of magazines for men, this is in fact no longer true. Nine men's monthlies, roughly equivalent in their readership profile to magazines like *Cosmopolitan* (which incidentally claims half a million male readers) and more or less entitled to the adjective 'girlie', sell between 110 000 (*Knave*) and 314 000 (*Fiesta*) copies each month. Once spurned by many advertisers, these magazines have come to be seen as respectable media, perhaps in default of anything else reaching that particular sector of the market.

Special-interest magazines

Are you a fly fisherman? Do you keep caged birds? Are you interested in gardening, woodworking, model aeroplanes, hot-rod cars, cycling? Do you play squash, golf, rugby, cricket? Whatever your interest, there is sure to be a magazine for you.

Special-interest and recreational magazines, of which there are about 500, range from the glossy camera and car periodicals to more humble and arcane publications with circulations of a thousand or two. They present few problems of choice to the advertiser or the media buyer, except where interests are so widely pursued – gardening and angling, for example – that the market begins to split. Advertisements for *Trout and Salmon*, for example, might not be suitable for the more downmarket *Angling Times*. But generally the advertiser will know whether he wants to buy space in one of these magazines; and in practice, as often as not, he will buy it direct, without the intervention of an agency or media buyer.

Trade, technical and business magazines

Much the same comment applies to this group. They serve highly specialist markets whose interests are predictable. Newspapers and magazines for grocers, doctors, chartered surveyors, electrical engineers, builders and solicitors all come into this category. Possibly what distinguishes them most as a group is the variety of ways in which they reach their readers. Some can be ordered from a newsagent in the usual way, or bought on subscription, for example the teachers' monthly *Junior Education*. Others arrive automatically as part of the subscription benefits of a professional body; an example is the *Pharmaceutical Journal*, which is published by the Pharmaceutical Society of Great Britain and goes weekly to all registered pharmacists (but is also available on subscription to 'outsiders'). Others again are, in a sense, professional freesheets, mailed to all members of a group or profession; the doctors' weekly *Pulse* is an example. The trade name for the last category is 'controlled circulation magazines'.

In the past twenty years there has been a huge growth in controlled circulation magazines. Some, which are little better than the local freesheets mentioned in the previous chapter with advertisements separated by editorial puffs written from public relations handouts, have tended to bring this sector of periodical publishing into disrepute and under suspicion. One difficulty is that professional people, to whom controlled circulation magazines are posted, have heavy enough mail – much of it unsolicited – anyway. Some publishers have tried to get round this problem and build up their credibility, by circulating their magazines only on request. But it is impossible to know how closely these magazines are actually read, and many advertisers treat them with reserve. An exception can be made for those which carry substantial employment advertising – though even here it may be only this section that is studied.

The trade press has a special function as a vehicle for linking wholesaler, retailer and retail customer for special promotions, cut-price offers and the like. Advertisers of retail products often take space in their trade papers to ensure that wholesalers and retailers are aware of these schemes and of supporting consumer advertising.

It is worth mentioning at this point the advertising business's own trade press which is essential reading for anyone who, for career or other reasons, wants to keep up with developments in a business where change is fast and frequent. The leading magazine is *Campaign*, which gives in-depth coverage of advertising, public relations and marketing, and is rich in up-to-date gossip about where people and accounts are moving. *UK Press Gazette* covers the press media, and in particular newspapers, mainly but not exclusively from the journalistic angle. Other titles include *Broadcast*, *Media Week*, and *Marketing Week*. Outside London, where they are fairly easily obtainable in areas where there are advertising or media offices, these periodicals have to be ordered from newsagents or by subscription.

Regional magazines

These monthlies, with titles like *Sussex Scene* and *Yorkshire Life*, have fairly modest circulations – 5000 to 10 000 is typical, though a few achieve more – but their readership is in the higher and more affluent social grades. They are widely used by advertisers of country property, upmarket cars, jewellery, country clothing and so on. They are useful media for advertisers in this slightly rarefied market.

Directories and year-books

Although they are not, strictly speaking, 'periodicals' within the definition given at the beginning of this chapter, directories and year-books have some of the same characteristics. They are published for most trades and professions, either by their organizations or by commercial publishers; there are also, of course, various regional and local directories.

Their interest to advertisers is in two distinct respects. Most of them carry advertisements and can be a useful way of reminding potential customers in a particular line of business about a company's products or services. Secondly, they are invaluable for compiling lists for direct-mail shots. By consulting the *Education Year*

Book, for example, it is possible to send a letter addressed by name to the head of every secondary school in the UK. The annual *Register of Pharmaceutical Chemists* would enable you to write to every registered pharmacist in the country (if, for example, you were offering an insurance policy of special interest to pharmacists) or to every chemist's shop (if you had a product to promote).

Regional and local directories are published variously by *Yellow Pages*, *Thomson's*, local newspaper groups and such bodies as chambers of trade. If you have ever used any of these to contact a supplier, you will have an idea of their usefulness to certain kinds of advertiser. In general, they are of major benefit to people whose services are needed in a hurry, such as electricians, plumbers, chimney-sweeps and tyre suppliers. You would be unlikely to choose, say, an accountant or a solicitor that way.

If you have a business telephone line, you get a standard listing in *Yellow Pages* free of charge. Display ads are paid for. Research suggests that well-displayed ads in directories pay for businesses which depend on 'distress' customers (that is, those with flat tyres or burst pipes) but less well for those which already have a high profile in their market. Putting it another way, if you run a village sweetshop you will be wasting your money. If you run a drain-clearing service, a directory ad may well be a major source of inquiries.

Advertising in periodicals

Periodicals, particularly those in the consumer field, offer advertisers a number of distinctive features:

high-quality colour printing in many cases

high readership per copy

a long readership life

strong editorial identity which spills over into the advertisements.

There is research evidence that, particularly with women's magazines, readers identify closely with the magazines they choose (as indeed, given the wide choice available, they have every opportunity to do with some accuracy) and 'trust' the advertisements as much as they do the editorial. This can, of course, be a snare for the unwary advertiser as well as an advantage for the careful one. In women's magazines, image is all; and an advertiser who has not judged the self-image of a reader of, say, *Woman's Journal* precisely enough may well be wasting his money on buying space. This is a field where circulation and readership figures by no means tell the whole story, and where the skilled media buyer can give invaluable help.

Readership – as distinct from circulation – is, however, a vital consideration to the magazine advertiser because, compared with newspapers, each copy of a magazine tends to be seen by a larger number of people; and people who are likely to be not merely other members of the family with or without purchasing power or interests in the relevant market, but prime purchasers in their own right. *Cosmopolitan*, for example, was showing nearly five women readers (six adult readers) per copy in 1985, according to the National Readership Survey, while *Over 21*, a little way down the market, showed over seven women readers (8.6 adults). NRS data also identifies readers by age and social class, marital and occupational status. Thus, the same 1985 survey showed that of *Cosmopolitan*'s women readers:

> 68 per cent were in the 15–34 age-bracket
>
> 62 per cent were in the top three social grades
>
> 44 per cent were single
>
> 45 per cent were working full-time

whereas with *Over 21*:

> 81 per cent were in the 15–34 age-bracket
>
> 52 per cent were in the top three social grades
>
> 59 per cent were single
>
> 51 per cent were working full-time.

The differences are reflected in another statistic: the median age of *Cosmopolitan* readers was 27.1 years, whereas that of *Over 21*'s was 22.4.

This contrast in readership profiles is even more marked if we look at the data for *Woman's Journal*, a monthly which, despite editorial changes in recent years, still retains a slightly well-upholstered, matronly image:

> 33 per cent were in the 15–34 age-bracket
>
> 65 per cent were in the top three social grades
>
> 25 per cent were single
>
> 38 per cent were working full-time
>
> and the median age of women readers was 43.2 years.

Woman's Journal, incidentally, showed 4.3 women readers per copy, with very little overspill into male readership.

Using readership figures

Readership figures are treated with some scepticism by some advertising people. For a start, the National Readership Survey covers only about a hundred magazine titles; and although NRS is by far the most scientifically respectable of the surveys, it suffers from distortions that are no fault of its own. Too many women's magazines have similar titles and similar cover layouts, and surveyed readers are sometimes understandably confused. Most magazines have a readership life that extends beyond one publication period – it may be a couple of months or more, for example, before a copy of *Over 21* gets round to its seventh reader – and this again distorts the survey findings. An alternative tool for the media planner is *Target Group Index*, published annually by the British Market Research Bureau, which identifies the media seen by users of various products and brands; but, like NRS, this covers only a limited number of magazines.

Many publishers fill in the gaps by commissioning their own surveys. While these are more reliable than they used to be – because the advertising world grows ever more sceptical, and ever more contemptuous of unsupportable claims – they are difficult to compare because not every publisher asks the same questions or interprets the results in the same way. Least useful of all to the advertiser (though they may have some benefits in terms of editorial decision-making) are surveys which are based on questionnaires inserted in a magazine and depending on reader response. Not only is the response likely to be small – readers expect to enjoy their magazines, not do their work for them – but it will also be statistically invalid.

Nevertheless, even if readership figures are to be treated with caution – those, at any rate, outside the range of NRS – magazines do offer the advertiser, by reason of their diversity, more precise targeting than either newspapers or television; provided the media buyer knows his stuff, there is less wastage. Against this and the other advantages mentioned earlier, two problems have to be set.

One is that magazines printed in colour, especially those in high-quality colour, have long lead times – the time between the copy date and publication. In the case of a monthly finished artwork may have to be with the publisher four or more months in advance of the cover month, which itself is one month after publication, and space must be booked several months in advance of the copy date. This makes magazine advertisements unacceptably inflexible for some advertisers – and a casual glance through a clutch of women's monthly magazines will confirm that much of the advertising is general rather than particular – say, Sainsbury's as a source of good food rather than Sainsbury's as retailers of particular products at specific prices, and brands of shoes rather than specific styles. At the same time, monthly publication makes magazines unsuitable for campaigns which depend upon the saturation effect – the intervals between ads are too long.

The second problem arises from the high proportion of advertising to editorial in the typical magazine. A typical proportion for a woman's monthly magazine is 60:40 in favour of advertising, and this inevitably means that not all the ads will be 'facing copy'. As magazines of this type are designed to be flipped through rather than read, there is a real danger that an ad may simply be overwhelmed. To some extent, this can be averted by paying a premium rate for a space facing copy (or 'facing matter', as it is known in the trade); but, even so, some advertisers worry about the volume of advertising in magazines. To be fair, it must also be said that, in general, adver-tisers prefer to buy space in a prosperous-looking periodical filled with advertising than in a thinner journal where, logically, their ad might be expected to receive closer attention.

Which space is effective?

There are a number of conventions about advertising in magazines – some of which, at least, seem to be little more than conventions. To a greater or lesser degree, advertisement rate cards reflect these. Such positions as 'facing matter', 'right-hand page' and 'front of book' attract premium rates, though not all magazines adopt the same policy. It is sometimes argued, with some conviction, that if an ad is good enough in visual and copy terms, it will be able to stand whatever position it finds itself in, and that if 'run of book' space is ordered (that is, space at the standard rate and the ad to fall wherever room can be found for it) it is as likely as not to fall in a premium space anyway. All this may well be true; the difficulty is that an agency often has to deal not in realities but in the vagaries of clients who may have their own prejudices. As with so much in advertising, the simple truth is that no one knows the relative pulling power of different magazine spaces, and attempts to establish some ground-rules by methods ranging from 'reading and noting' surveys (based on field research) to cameras which track the eye movements of typical readers have not so far come up with any reliable guidance.

In the trade, technical and business field, different readership criteria apply, and the way in which magazines are read and used also affects their value as advertising media. Let us suppose that there is a professional body called the Chartered Institute of Refuse Disposers, with a membership of 7000, and that every month each member receives, as a membership right, a copy of *Chartered Refuse Disposal*. To a manufacturer of relevant equipment, it may seem encouraging that everyone with an interest in the market will see his advertisement. But of course, not all members of the Chartered Institute are in a position to influence decisions on the buying of equipment. Many will be students in their first jobs; more will be assistants, deputy assistants or assistant deputies. Some will be retired. At an optimistic estimate, perhaps 700 of the readers of *Chartered Refuse Disposal* will be in a position to do something about the advertiser's message.

This may not matter. If the price of space is right and gets you the attention of all the top dogs in the business, it will be worth while – and, as a bonus, you establish your name with all those underlings who will one day, in their turn, become top dogs. But the example illustrates an important consideration for advertisers who are not in the mass market: it's the *quality* of the readership that counts. Quality, in this context, means not necessarily position in the hierarchy but the ability to control expenditure. No Fellow of the Chartered Institute of Refuse Disposers is going to waste his time (we must hope) deciding which among the many makers of dustbin bags is going to get his authority's custom. He will delegate the job to a junior. So if you make dustbin bags and are thinking of advertising in *Chartered Refuse Disposal*, you might well think again. And it will be surprising if some enterprising publisher is not putting out a controlled circulation magazine which goes to actual buyers in the refuse disposal business and which could be a better showplace for your ad. Conversely, of course, if you were making capital equipment, especially if it had some revolutionary feature, you might feel the need to influence those at the top. All this illustrates a very basic 'horses for courses' rule, and yet it is surprising how often, looking through the trade and professional press, one sees space being wasted carrying messages to people who are not in a position to do anything about them.

Many magazines extend their relationships with their advertisers beyond the mere selling of space into various support and marketing services, which can be particularly valuable to a small company without a marketing department of its own. These services range from reader reply – in which the reader sends in a request for details of the products or services he indicates – to such things as in-store merchandising, public relations, and exhibition promotions. Whether these are add-on services or simply inducements to advertise, they are often worth considering. On the other hand, advertisers should be wary of attempts to sell them advertising space against editorial mentions, a practice fairly common in the trade press. Magazines which do this habitually are always recognized in their respective trades and are therefore downgraded in authority and integrity. Editorial mentions which are offered *after* space has been bought are, of course, a different matter.

5 The other media

Broadcasting and press advertising is so predominant – accounting, in Britain, for roughly 90 per cent of annual advertising expenditure – that it is difficult to find a satisfactory term for the remaining media which include outdoor advertising, the cinema, direct mail and a variety of others. The term 'minor media' is sometimes used – but rather unfairly, because there is nothing minor about a £140 million industry, which is the size of the outdoor advertising spend each year in the UK. However, it is true to say that these media are very rarely used on their own, but act as back-up to television or press campaigns.

Outdoor advertising

This term covers not only poster sites – the dominant sector – but also advertisements on the sides and backs of buses and taxis, in bus shelters, on railway stations, in shopping malls, at sports grounds, and so on. Although in fact some outdoor advertising – that in bus shelters, for example – is sited in places where people have time to read copy, the general rule is to keep the outdoor advertising message simple: a brand name or logo, a crisp headline, a clear, easily read image.

There are about 175 000 poster sites in Britain, mainly on the approach roads to the big cities and in city centres. They come in various sizes, based on multiples of the double-crown (762×508 mm) sheet. Thus, there are 4, 12, 16, 32 and 48-sheet sites, together with some 3500 extra-large 'supersites'. The numbers break down as follows:

Table 5.1. *Numbers and sizes of poster sites in the UK, 1985*

Size	Number
4-sheet (portrait)	77 000
12-sheet (landscape)	1 500
16-sheet (portrait)	51 000
32-sheet (landscape)	7 000
48-sheet (landscape)	37 000

Obviously, this multiplicity of sizes causes some headaches to those planning the use of poster sites, and the 32-sheet site, which was always something of an oddity, is in decline. The 12-sheet site, in the same proportions as the 48-sheet, is a fairly recent innovation and is used mainly in urban pedestrian areas.

No one likes posters more than the people in advertising, who find in them outlets for creative flair, ingenuity and dramatic effect. Nowhere else in advertising can art directors find such a large canvas whose use may indeed alter – and often improve – a whole environment. There are no legal limits on the product categories that may be advertised on posters, which presents an added attraction to advertisers proscribed by television. The result is that some posters, especially for drink and cigarettes, have achieved perhaps the highest and purest forms of advertising art; while dramatic campaigns, like that for Araldite adhesive in the early 1980s in which a real car was stuck on a hoarding, pushed the poster business towards new adventures.

In general, poster advertising is bought long-term, though within the period of booking the posters themselves may be changed. One striking use of this facility has been in London, where, on a series of sites strategically chosen along commuter routes, posters were changed weekly to announce a forthcoming major programme from London Weekend Television. The more normal interval for poster changes is one month. Sites are booked either on an annual and more-or-less permanent basis (TC – 'till countermanded') or for a three-month season.

In Britain, poster advertising is almost entirely in the hands of two sales companies, which offer various packages of sites giving national, regional, TV regional or local coverage. These packages are known as PSCs (pre-selected campaigns). The printing, distribution and posting of posters dictates a fairly long lead time between the planning of a campaign and its execution, so that outdoor advertising is not a flexible medium. As the larger posters are produced in separate pieces which have to be matched together, printing quality, especially in the matching of colour, is critical. But posters do achieve good coverage and give a repeated message, which accounts for their appeal as relatively inexpensive reminders of television campaigns.

Transport advertising

After posters, transport is the second largest sector of out-door advertising. It includes advertisements on the sides and ends of buses, cards inside, posters on railway and underground stations and the cards inside the coaches on the underground. There is a great deal of flexibility in the packages available so that, while a national advertiser could, if he wished, get his message on to the majority of buses in the country, a trader in a Bakerloo Line suburb could run a modest and effective campaign by using tube cards in the appropriate trains. The form and content of these ads vary. You can afford to put quite a lot of detail on the back of a bus which is going to be stared at by following motorists, and on bus and tube cards; passengers at underground stations (though not those on esca-lators) have time to read copy; but a bus side is similar, in terms of readability, to a roadside poster.

A more exotic form of transport advertising is to have a whole bus painted in company livery and decorated with appropriate slogans and brand names. It's showy, but the results are as yet un-researched.

Cinema

Before television, the cinema was the only advertising medium offering both colour and movement, and consequently it has a long advertising history. Who, of those old enough to have seen them, can forget those primitive ads for Acme wringers, those matrons restoring their energy with Australian burgundy, Raymond Glendenning interviewing sports heroes for Players, and those stills of the local greengrocer's with the catch-all voiceover, 'Buy your fresh fruit and vegetables at this shop'? Much has changed in the film exhibition industry, and one of the changes has been the increased sophistication of cinema advertising. There are a number of reasons for this. Cinema commercials offer their producers far higher standards of picture and sound than television. Their audiences, who tend to be film loyalists, are visually more aware and demanding. Film commercials are free from the restraints of time that affect television, and free also from restrictions on the advertising of certain products. The audience is captive and attentive, provided that the commercial competes in quality with the programmed films. Many of the innovative ideas that we now take for granted in television commercials were pioneered in front of the more critical cinema audience, though complete commercials as such do not, on the whole, travel easily to and fro between cinema and TV screen.

The monetary value of cinema advertising in relation to the whole advertising business is minuscule: in 1983 it accounted for 0.5 per cent of total advertising expenditure in the UK. But this is a deceptive statistic, because the cinema scores very well with the age-group of the lightest television viewers: the 15–24-year-olds. Well over half the regular cinema audience is in this age-group. This is also the sector of the population with overall the largest amount of disposable income, making it a target for advertisers of a wide range of products and services, from manufacturers of designer jeans to the managers of High Street banks.

In the 1980s the cinema audience in Britain has staged a mild recovery, culminating in 1985 in a sharp increase as a result of the British Film Year promotion; but of course it is now a minority form of entertainment, in competition for the disposable income of young adults with pubs, night-clubs, discos and sports complexes. There are about 700 cinemas in Britain, with about twice that number of separate screens. Screen time is bought in an almost infinite variety of ways. Commercials can be booked to travel as part of complete programmes (notably with family programmes of the Walt Disney type), by individual cinemas or geographical groups, or by a complete national or regional circuit. So the cinema has something to offer every kind of advertiser, from the High Street trader (the stills-with-voiceovers are still there, though these days they are more likely to be advertising an Indian restaurant than a greengrocer) to the national manufacturer.

Direct mail

Direct mail, not to be confused with direct response, is direct-to-your-door advertising through the post. Strictly speaking, direct mail is regarded in the advertising business as 'below the line' – that is, not direct advertising proper; but the distinction is a blurred one and is more technical than real.

Direct mail is expensive, mainly because of the cost of postage – despite generous discounts available from the Post Office for partially-sorted bulk mailings. It is therefore used to generate continuing and substantial sales, either of a variety of goods, as with a mail order store, or of a series, as with a book or record club. Success in this field depends on two factors. The material sent through the post, whether in the form of a letter or a brochure, must be attractive enough to survive its first few minutes in the recipient's hands. Secondly, it must go to the right recipients. Even the most careful attention to the quality of the message and of the mailing list cannot fulfil these criteria completely, and it is estimated that almost 20 per cent of direct mail is thrown away unread. There is no estimate for the amount that is put on one side to be read later and subsequently forgotten, put behind the clock until spring-cleaning or simply read but not acted upon.

Direct mail is something of a mystery to those not engaged in it, and perhaps even to those involved. It defies belief – for me, at any rate – that anyone is going to wade through the reams of verbiage, picked out in garish colours and hideous type faces, that regularly arrive from certain large organizations; or that anyone is going to be deceived by the crude personalization which invites me, say, to consider how the neighbours are going to react when they see me driving off from 35 Acacia Avenue in my brand-new Ford Fiesta; or that anyone has the time to fiddle with draw tickets, 'YES' and 'NO' stickers and all the rest of it. Yet I have been assured by a direct-mail practitioner that the more a recipient has to do when he receives direct mail, the better, and that the instinct of most of us to keep a direct-mail letter short and crisp is quite misguided. The minimum length for a sales letter, it seems, is two pages – with most of the second page filled – and the really professional operators refuse to make do with fewer than four, backing the letter with sundry other bits and pieces.

The quality of a mailing list depends on the accurate targeting of potential buyers of the product you have to sell. Hundreds of lists are available from mailing houses, pinpointing specific trades and professions, occupiers of specific types of houses, people with specific buying habits, and so on. Lists can be bought for use by the client's own sales operation, or the job can be farmed out entirely to a mailing house. Direct mail is used extensively for industrial as well as domestic sales, and precise lists are available in this area. The identification of markets by type of housing, for domestic direct mail purposes, is discussed in the next chapter.

Direct response advertising appears in the press (notably in the Sunday colour magazines) and to a limited extent on television using either a short freepost address or a freefone number. It is a type of press or TV advertising rather than a medium in its own right. But the responses can be used to build up or augment the advertiser's own mailing list for future offers.

And the rest . . .

Beer-mats, hot-air balloons, showcards, window displays, tin trays, doormats, mugs, jotters, pens, parking-meter stickers, display vehicles for exhibitions and trade shows . . . all are forms of 'below the line' advertising which are used mainly to keep brand names before the public. Some, like the card advertising someone's cough mixture which tells you whether the chemist's is open or shut, are classified as 'point of sale' material. Others, like the shopkeeper's pencil with a brand-name on it, could be classed as a modest 'business gift'. Just occasionally one of these devices is used in an imaginative way that brings it out of the rut; for example, the East Anglian insurance brokers Smith and Pinching have a hot-air balloon which they operate for publicity purposes, and the balloon logo is used in all their advertising, with copy that extends the theme.

A.—6

6 The market

The essence of advertising is that it is specifically aimed at someone – or, rather, at a collection of someones who are the potential consumers or who (with 'opinion-forming' ads, for instance) will modify their attitudes or behaviour in the light of the message they have received. All advertisements, however good their copy or striking their artwork, however inspired their casting or talented their direction, have first to cross this terrain between advertiser and consumer, and if they do not succeed in this they do not succeed at all.

This is something too easily forgotten in some sectors of the advertising business: by the client who forgets that advertisements are for consumers, not to impress fellow managers; by the agency more keen to produce work that will win admiration in the profession than work that will sell product; by the individual creative director whose first priority is to make his mark. One of the advantages of the agency system is that it introduces some checks and balances, as well as compensating personalities, into the complex business of creating effective advertising. The more people are involved in a campaign, the less chance there is of someone drifting away on an ego-trip.

But first, before a word of copy is written and before the first stroke of a visualizer's felt tip pen, comes the question of that gulf between advertiser and audience. It can be seen as a problem of navigation, of getting from one place to another. The advertiser knows his own position (or, sometimes, he knows where he wants his own position to be); the problem is to find, first of all, where the consumer is. Advertising is too expensive for people to flail around in the dark hoping for a lucky strike. Advertisers, agencies and the individual media are therefore concerned with the precise identification of markets, and with analysing how people in those markets behave, what are their age, sex, social grade, lifestyle, tastes and habits. A vast amount of expenditure, largely invisible to the world outside advertising and marketing, goes into these investigations, and the language in which the findings are expressed makes up a large part of advertising jargon.

Keeping tabs

The questions extend, it seems, almost to infinity. What is the proportion of 15–24-year-olds in the population of the UK? (The answer is 18 per cent.) How many women readers of 19 magazine are in the 15–24 age-bracket? (Answer: 73 per cent, which is to say 478150 readers a month in the period January–June 1985.) Are housewives brand loyal when they buy butter or breakfast cereals? (No. About four-fifths of them buy more than one brand.) Do adults plagued with indigestion always turn to the same remedy? (About two-thirds do.) How many people watched the *Royal Variety Performance* on ITV on Sunday, 1 December 1985? (No fewer than 15.90 million.) Was that the biggest TV audience of the week? (No. The *Royal Variety Performance* came fifth, beaten by the twice-weekly episodes of BBC1's *EastEnders* and ITV's *Coronation Street*.) And so it goes: the people we are, the TV programmes we watch, the extent to which we watch television at all, our habits of film going, radio listening, reading, playing games, the food we eat, the brands we choose, the degree of brand loyalty we display, the newspapers and magazines we buy, our consumption of whisky and cigarettes, the places we choose to save our money, the places we choose for our holidays – truly, all human life is there, researched and analysed and updated annually if not more often, and available, sometimes for free and sometimes at a price, to advertisers who want to put their finger on us, not as individuals but as members of a specific market – or, rather, as members of a number of specific markets.

When the adman speaks of buying 'demographics' rather than of buying space or time, he is talking about buying slices of the market which will be watching that space or viewing at that time. Salesmen of advertising space in a newspaper are not really selling 20 centimetres by two columns on a particular page; they are selling a piece of the attention of people of the age, sex and social status who read that newspaper. If you pay a premium rate to get your ad into the break in the middle of *Coronation Street* in every ITV region (which is difficult and expensive, but can be done) you will be paying for the attention of over 16 million people, something like half the mass market. (But they will tend to be over 35, and in the lower half of the social grading.)

The slice of the market at which an advertisement is aimed is called the target group or target audience. The starting-point in defining the target audience is by reference to age, sex and class.

Age

The age-groups normally used in advertising are:

    −15
    15–24
    25–34
    35–55
    55+

In general terms (for individual advertisers of, say, teddy-bears or shopping trolleys, the criteria are different) the age sector of most interest is the 15–34 group. This combines the maximum amount of disposable income, after obligations have been met, with the maximum pressure to follow style and fashion, to set up home and build up an environment of consumer durables. It is no accident that most of the women's monthly magazines strive hard to appeal to this market – with great success, as shown by their readerships among 15–34-year-old women: *Company*, 83 per cent; *Look Now*, 90 per cent; *19*, 87 per cent; *Over 21*, 81 per cent. But for the first ten years of this period, people are light viewers of television and light readers of newspapers, and this explains a number of curiosities of the advertising business, including the survival of so many women's magazines and the relative prosperity, in relation to the amount spent, of cinema advertising.

Characteristics of 15–34-year-olds include:

> They go out more, to the cinema and the theatre, to discos and pubs, for meals, and on family outings when they have children.

They buy more clothes and replace them more often.

They are more experimental with food and drink.

They are vulnerable to changes in fashion and style.

They pursue more interests outside the immediate family.

Beyond 34, and into what many people may be horrified to find is regarded in advertising as middle age, a different pattern emerges: the rich get richer and the poor get poorer. Professionals are on the threshold of the bigger earnings that they have slaved to achieve; they become bank managers, senior partners, head teachers, hospital consultants. They may well have felt left behind in the 15–34 spending bonanza; but now they begin to come into their own. They start to buy wine knowledgeably instead of simply snatching a known name off the supermarket shelf. They take their motoring upmarket. They can afford to indulge in expensive cameras or audio equipment, fashion bedding or furnishings. They are the people at whom the quality Sunday supplements are aimed. Women who can afford it dress more expensively, knowing that as the body's muscles sag they need to be packaged more carefully.

Meanwhile, wage-earners are in an entirely different position. Their earnings, relative to the cost of living, have reached a plateau. At the same time they face increased outgoings, largely because of the demands of growing children. In the current state of society, they face the prospect of possible unemployment as they grow older or of an expensive move to find new work. They tend to look to television as their main, and perhaps only, means of entertainment and recreation. They 'count the pennies'. While a 35–55-year-old housewife in the lower social grades may try 'something a bit different' for tea, she is a more conservative purchaser of food products than her younger sister, and her husband a more conservative eater. When they can afford to, this age-group may follow social trends (such as the swing from ale to lager, or new styles of mass market clothing), but they do not initiate them.

The over-55s exhibit an extension of the differences between the haves and have-nots. Prosperous over-55s are extensive consumers of travel, holidays, new cars, clothes and luxuries generally. At the other end of the wealth scale, the over-55s consume less over virtually the whole range of products and services – except, notably, for newspapers (which they read avidly up to the age of about 65) and television (which, as they grow older, they watch almost obsessively, including children's programmes).

Sex

The population of the UK is made up as follows:

Children (to age 15):	26 per cent
Men:	35 per cent
Women:	39 per cent

Of the total population, 32 per cent are classed as 'housewives' in the sense used in advertising: the person who accepts day-to-day responsibility for running the home and caring for the children. This does not necessarily imply marriage or the presence of a partner, though it tends to be forgotten, under the assaults of the women's movement, that the basic household unit in Britain (and, indeed, throughout the developed world) is one in which the main bread-winner is a male married to a female lesser breadwinner who is also a 'housewife'.

Although women have, statistically, less earning power than men, they make the major purchasing decisions over a large range of pro-ducts, including such items as men's clothes, but generally exclud-ing 'technical' purchases other than for domestic appliances. In food products, housewife purchases account for 80 per cent or more of sales.

The difference between men and women in the readership of newspapers or the watching of television is not significant over each medium as a whole, but specific newspapers and TV programmes show variations. For example, the readership of the *Financial Times* is 74 per cent male, against 55 per cent for national newspapers in general; while women watch more TV drama than men.

Class

It is a cliché (not uttered so frequently by those who have spent any time in French or American society) that Britain is peculiarly obsessed with social class. Whatever the truth of this may be, class (or, as advertising people prefer to call it, social grade) is a convenient way of identifying markets.

The social grade classification most commonly used in advertising and marketing is one developed for the National Readership Survey. It is something of a blunt instrument, and no one would claim that it is an entirely satisfactory index; but although there has been much discussion concerning devising a better one, no more useful system has emerged. At least the NRS classification provides a convenient shorthand and has the merit of being very widely used, so that comparisons across a range of data are easily made.

Table 6.1. *Social grades in the UK*

Grade	Occupation of head of household*	Percentage of population
A	Higher managerial, administrative and professional (e.g. the director of a public company, a senior civil servant)	3.1
B	Intermediate managerial, administrative and professional (e.g. a works manager, the head of a secondary school)	13.4
C1	Supervisory, clerical and junior managerial, administrative and professional (e.g. a senior secretary, an assistant teacher in a state school)	22.3
C2	Skilled manual (e.g. a motor engineer, a rail driver)	31.2
D	Semi-skilled and unskilled manual (e.g. a coal-miner, a shop assistant)	19.1
E	Those at the lowest levels of subsistence (e.g. casual labourers, state pensioners, widows, the unemployed)	10.9

*The 'head of the household' is the earner of the largest part of a household's income.

There are a number of objections to the too slavish use of these gradings. They beg such questions as the following: whether, in a mobile society, people moving up or down the structure carry their original tastes and lifestyles with them or adopt those of their new grading; what happens in the case of a headmaster (B) married to a C1 assistant teacher when, as is usual, the wife makes most of the purchasing choices? In practice, these objections are largely invalidated because it is rare for *individual* social gradings to be used. Advertisers speak of the *quality* (ABC1) and the *mass* (C2D) markets.

Incidentally, the increases and decreases in the NRS social grades between 1979 and 1984 tend to confirm what is said by politicians about the increasing polarization of British society:

Table 6.2.　*Changes in social grades as a percentage of the population of the UK population, 1979–84*

Social grade	Change, per cent
A	Nil
B	+1
C1	−½
C2	−1½
D	−2
E	+2½

The official government *Census of Population* uses a more sophisticated classification by occupation, dividing the population into 'socio-economic groups' of occupations with broadly comparable characteristics. These groups do not define markets; however, they need to be understood by anyone in advertising and marketing making use of government statistics in their research:

Table 6.3.　*Census of Population, UK: Socio-economic groups*

Number	Occupation
SEG1	Employers and managers in large establishments
SEG2	Employers and managements in small establishments
SEG3	Professional workers, self-employed
SEG4	Professional workers, employees
SEG5i	Ancillary workers and artists
SEG5ii	Foremen and supervisors, non-manual
SEG6	Junior non-manual workers
SEG7	Personal service workers
SEG8	Foremen and supervisors, manual
SEG9	Skilled manual workers
SEG10	Semi-skilled manual workers
SEG11	Unskilled manual workers
SEG12	Own account workers, non-professional
SEG13	Farmers – employers and managers
SEG14	Farmers – own account
SEG15	Agricultural workers
SEG16	Members of armed forces
SEG17	Inadequately described occupations

Getting the market into focus

When you have identified someone by age, sex and social grade, you have gone some way towards zooming in on him, but not far enough for most advertising purposes. Such terms as 'ABC1 women aged 15–24' certainly describes a sector of the population, but it is a large sector with diverse financial status, habits, tastes and lifestyles. It includes, for example, several members of the Royal Family as well as the daughters of a state schoolteacher living in, let us say, Tees-side. We can move into sharper focus by adding to the definition 'ABC1 women aged 15–24' a 'who' qualification: '. . . who follow slimming diets'; '. . . who make their own cakes'; '. . . who do the household grocery shopping'; and so on. This kind of information is available from various sources: the government's annual *Social Trends* is a mine of information on buying habits, while more specific detail can be obtained from such organizations as Mintel, Target Group Index and the Economist Intelligence Unit. The identification of a target group usually arises from information supplied from these sources, *plus*, if the advertiser can afford it, some market research related to the specific product or market, *plus* intuition or, if you like, imagination.

Round about 1980, for example, Beecham Foods felt the need to reposition their glucose drink, Lucozade, in the market-place. Sales had been falling, for a number of market reasons which do not concern us here, and it was decided to play down Lucozade as a drink for convalescence and emphasize an 'in-health' message. The target audience for this new message was identified as 'active women between the ages of 18 and 35 who care about the health and well-being of themselves and their children'. Now, you do not identify this audience by asking people if they care for their health and well-being; of course they do. So into the strategy that led to the revival of this long-established-brand drink went a certain amount of intuition that could not be validated by research.

Intuition can, of course, fail. It did so spectacularly when the compact disc was introduced in 1983. The compact disc was billed as 'perfect sound which will last for ever', and the original launch was aimed at the top end of the audio market. Its digitally recorded sound, it was claimed, was non-degradable however many times the disc was played. You could spill a glass of wine on the surface and there would be no damage. Since compact discs cost more than twice as much as conventional LPs, there was some sense in appealing to the better-off audio enthusiast. People must expect to pay for the much-advertised absence of wow, flutter and rumble.

In fact, the pitch, in both advertising and aural terms, turned out to be wrong. Compact discs, the enthusiasts complained, gave a sound-quality that was almost *too* perfect, soul-less. They preferred the 'reality' of the conventional disc, scratches, pops, clicks and all. (Cynics might suspect that the perfection of CD removed opportunities for owners to demonstrate the sensitivity of their equipment by adjusting tone and balance controls themselves, in the same way as, in the 1950s, ready-to-cook cake-mixes were thought to devalue the housewife's contribution to cake-making.) The result was that in 1985 the makers of CD equipment shifted their marketing strategy to the middle market, where possession of the latest equipment counts for more than the sound that comes out of it. But the two-year false start certainly inhibited the take-up of CD.

North of Watford

National advertisers and their agents also have to consider regional variations in the market. What sells well in New York City may not go down at all well in Hazelton, Pa. In Britain, the dividing-line between the two nations is traditionally (and quite unjustifiably) Watford. In fact, there are quite wide regional variations between all regions of Britain, faithfully charted for the curious by such government publications as the *National Food Survey* and *Social Trends*. For example, the English eat almost twice as much fresh fruit as the Scots – who, however, eat markedly higher amounts of potatoes and bread. The Welsh occupy the middle consumption positions over a wide range of foods, but they eat less cheese than either English or Scots. This information can, of course, be interpreted in at least two ways: does the Welsh cheese market need to be developed, or is it too small to bother with? Either way, if you were selling cheese in Wales you would need to consider the question.

Change and renewal

The market is in a constant state of movement, vulnerable as it is to a whole range of external influences. The mechanics by which these influences work are of great interest to advertisers, not only because they reveal how consumers behave but also because use can be made of them in selling, launching or repositioning products. This is perhaps best illustrated by examples.

The case of the fish finger

The example of the fish finger shows how a new product, assiduously promoted, can affect not only a nation's eating habits but also the equipment of its kitchens.

Before 1955, fish was among the least favourite foods for consumption at home. People, particularly children, didn't much like the taste and liked even less fiddling about with the skin and the bones. Yet fish is a nutritious, healthy food available in abundance. In 1955, Birdseye put the first fish fingers on the market in Britain. They revolutionized children's taste almost overnight, and within five years 12 000 tonnes of fish fingers were being produced. For 1985 the figure was 41 000 tonnes – a £95 million market, 10 per cent of Britain's total fish consumption, of which Birdseye were market leaders with 50 per cent. And the fish finger had also spawned a range of other frozen fish products, spanning all ages and social grades.

All done by advertising. As it happened, the first fish fingers went on sale in the same month as the start of commercial television in Britain. TV has always seen the thrust of fish finger advertising; and Captain Birdseye, who made his début in 1967, has been featured in no fewer than 35 different commercials since then, with a three-year interval during which he was rested – and sales slumped.

What Birdseye and their rivals had done was to rescue fish from a rapid decline in popularity, and at the same time solve the perennial problem of the wet fish trade, which lay in distribution. But they had also done something else: they had brought frozen food out of the luxury and into the popular class, and set the scene for a dramatic change in the way British housewives bought and stored food. In 1955 less than 3 per cent of British homes had fridges, and virtually none had freezers. Today, 96 per cent have fridges and 70 per cent have freezers. Hand in hand with this change have gone the concepts of one-stop shopping, the weekly instead of the daily shop, bulk buying and, of course, a vast improvement in the hygiene and diet of British families.

Fish was an established, if less than popular, part of the British diet; but the fish finger, which you didn't have to use at once and on which all the tricky work such as filleting had already been done, was an entirely new product. The challenge that Birdseye were taking on in 1955 cannot be overestimated. They had decided to target their advertising on children – wisely, as it turned out, because children polish off half the fish fingers eaten. They were therefore in the position of selling to children something that children were known to dislike. They had chosen the unfamiliar term 'fish fingers', which it was suspected might cause market resistance. And they opted to use the then unknown quantity (in Britain) of television as the spearhead of the advertising campaign. Triumphantly, all these gambles paid off – but there must have been some raw nerves in the Birdseye offices in September 1955 when the first ads went out.

No doubt there were other factors, not all of them attributable to the marketing and advertising expertise of the Birdseye team, at work in Birdseye's success. In the mid-1950s, the children of the post-war birth-rate bulge were at the age where their mothers were desperate to find attractive, nutritious food which would be eaten without protest. The fact that the product was advertised on television gave it a certain novelty and glamour. Britain was at that time coming out of the grey, austerity-ridden post-war years and, with full employment, the launch price of fish fingers, at 1s 8d (just over 8p) for a packet of six, was pitched about right for a ready-to-heat family meal. Mothers were going to work in large numbers – this was the period when the term 'latch-key children' was coined – and fish fingers had an obvious appeal for them. Birdseye, in short, had a product that was exactly right for its moment.

The case of the cover-up

With all the research and strategic planning in the world, however, advertising is not infallible, as the story of Persil Automatic shows.

Persil Automatic was one of the well-established brands of low-sud powders for front-loading automatic washing machines. Heavy TV advertising – virtually all detergent advertising is on television – had given it a high profile, but by the early 1980s there were problems. The so-called 'biological' powders containing enzymes, such as Ariel, were gaining a lead. Increasing amounts of domestic laundry consisted of synthetic or partly synthetic materials, which were washed at lower temperatures. Persil Automatic's problem was that it was less effective at these lower temperatures than the biologicals. The answer put forward was 'New System' Persil Automatic, a biological powder; and, with heavy promotion, the new brand took off.

It was not long before complaints began to come in from members of the public and from doctors. People with distressing skin conditions such as contact dermatitis – of whom there are large numbers – had relied on the original Persil Automatic as the least irritant of the automatic washing powders. Using 'New System', they found that their condition deteriorated, in some cases very severely and painfully. Lever, the makers of Persil, protested in vain that the new product had been thoroughly tested, as no doubt it had, and that there was no reason why 'New System' should irritate the skin. For a time it looked as if Lever were going to hold out. However, within eighteen months, after a number of damaging press stories, pressure from a group of doctors, and the intervention into the UK market of the Swiss manufacturer of non-allergenic detergent for front-loading automatics, there was an announcement: Old Persil was coming back, alongside 'New System', but it would be called 'Original Non-Biological'.

In the re-launch of 'Original Non-Biological' Persil we find an example of a market which had been very closely identified indeed: C1, C2 and D housewives with front-loading automatic washing machines *who suffered, or had members of the household who suffered, from skin allergies.*

Fashion, style, trend, image

Fish fingers appealed to housewives who perceived a *need* for nutritious, convenient food which children would eat and enjoy. New System Persil Automatic attracted housewives who felt the need to get the washing completely free from stains and discoloration. Such needs can be assessed by reference to the market. But in a developed industrial society, where most people already have the necessities of life, it is necessary to stimulate demand (and perhaps improve the gaiety of the nation) by moving beyond what is necessary to what is desirable.

Looked after, a modern car will last at least ten years. Furniture can last a lifetime. There are plenty of couples past their golden weddings who are still sleeping on their original marriage beds. Those of us who wear suits only rarely are often shocked at the image in the mirror when we drag out the old suit for some special occasion. In practical terms, at my own rate of suit-wearing, one would have lasted me for the past fifteen years and will last me for the next twenty. In fact, as any jumble sale reveals, few clothes these days get worn out.

All this presents problems to the manufacturer. There are two ways round the difficulty. One is to make an entirely new product – the compact disc player, for example. The other is to rely on one of the four words heading this section to change the taste of the market.

A consumer society is one in which people feel the need to fit in with trends, to identify and make statements about themselves by their choice of dress, furnishings, furniture and so on. One of the greatest social changes that has come over Western societies in the past hundred years has been that the ability to respond to fashion has spread from the upper and middle classes to virtually everyone. A century ago, for example – and well into living memory in some areas – the normal dress for working-class children was 'cut-me-down' adult clothes. No one would have believed, then, that it would be possible to make a living out of mass-marketed clothes for children. In those days, clothes were worn, or passed on, until they fell apart. Much the same was true of furniture: when you set up home, you made purchases for life. Our grandfathers would have thought it incredible – and profligate – that we should refurnish our homes simply because we had grown tired of the old stuff.

Fashion, style, trend and image rarely originate in advertising. They need reference points in the real world; what happens is that advertising people read the cues provided by the rag trade, the music industry, films and so on. There was a simple example of this when, in the 1960s, colour television was introduced in Britain. At once, TV presenters began sporting highly coloured and patterned clothes, and within a few months men's clothes in particular had taken on a new peacock style. Similarly, set designers on TV celebrated their liberation from black and white, and their extravagance with colour was soon reflected in home decoration and furnishings.

Getting the facts

The market is like shingle at the seaside, in a state of constant movement. Fashion, style, trend, image, the introduction of new products and processes, changes in the prosperity of different age-ranges and social grades, even the weather and the political climate, all influence what people buy. The advertising business is interested both in general trends, which are monitored by various annual government surveys and by commercial organizations like Mintel, and in trends affecting specific product ranges. For example, the manufacturers of our fictitious chocolate bar *Chase* need to know about the amount of disposable income among their target group, the amount of that income spent on confectionery, and how expenditure rates between the different confectionery product lines. The answers to these questions are found by **quantitative research**, which is concerned with finding out how many people make certain purchases, how often, of which sex, what age and what social group.

Quantitative research is based on sampling, on the principle that if you take a sample of people within a given target group, their answers to your questions can be extrapolated to relate to the whole group. The most familiar examples of the technique to most people are the TV weekly audience tables and the various surveys of voting intentions. Although the principle is simple enough, practice is nowhere near as easy. In the first place, the sample has to be carefully assembled so that it is truly representative of the whole target group. Secondly, the phrasing of the questions is critical. Apart from the obvious hazards like ambiguity or leading the respondent, the responses must pinpoint precisely the topic at issue. This accounts for what sometimes seems, to the outsider, the unnecessarily complex sets of questions that are asked by field workers in market research.

The science of quantitative research has been practised and refined over many years, becoming increasingly sophisticated; although it is not infallible, it is a reliable, and indeed indispensable, tool. Readers who recall various mishaps that have befallen electoral surveys, which are conducted on the same basis, may have twinges of doubt – but it must be remembered that electoral surveys ask questions about respondents' *future* intentions – something that would not be done in research for advertising or marketing purposes – and are corrupted by the difference (which, since it varies widely, cannot be allowed for) between the number of people who intend (or *say* they intend) to vote in a particular way and the number who actually turn out to do so.

Quantitative research produces figures, more or less crude according to the sophistication of the exercise; however, unless conducted on a financially prohibitive scale it cannot provide all the information on the market that an advertiser may need. For fine tuning, use is often made of **qualitative research**, whose aim is to explore perceptions and attitudes among a small, but carefully chosen, group in the target area. The most common form of qualitative research is a group discussion involving up to ten or a dozen people, with the interviewer acting as discussion leader. An alternative, but lengthier and therefore more expensive, approach is to conduct individual 'in depth' interviews. The question whether people are more or less inhibited face to face than in group discussion is an open one.

Either way, the proceedings are recorded, and significant quotations from the discussion are later used as the basis of the research report. Qualitative research might be used before an advertising strategy is drawn up, in order to investigate the standing of the product in the market, or as a means of testing trial advertisements, or during and after a campaign to check on how well the campaign objectives have been met.

Case histories: 2

When we last met the makers of Chase chocolate bars, do-it-yourself suppliers Taplow's and generator manufacturers Beaver, they had each identified their respective problem and were wondering what to do next. As we return to them, they are about to consider the implications of the market.

Chase

From the three advertising agencies invited to pitch for the business of re-launching Chase, the company chose ABCD. ABCD had the account for another of the company's products, and there was a strong feeling in the marketing department that Chase needed an agency which understood the company and its history. (Equally validly, it might have been argued that what was needed was a fresh approach that was *not* informed by a previous relationship.)

ABCD recognized correctly that the revival of Chase's fortunes was important to the company not only in revenue terms but also in terms of the company's self-image and its reputation in the confectionery trade as a whole. So whatever the new image of Chase turned out to be, it would have to be sold heavily to the trade as well as to the consumer. To some extent the story was not the revival of Chase but the revival of its manufacturers. This was the measure of the assignment.

The message from Chase's own research, described earlier, was clear enough. The bar was seen as old-fashioned, appealing to a declining band of chocolate bar consumers. This might not necessarily be a bad thing; another way of interpreting the same finding was that Chase suggested traditional virtues – a good, solid taste that you could recognize, value for money, pleasant childhood associations. But (so went the argument round the tables in the ABCD offices) you had to be over 55 to get any pleasant childhood associations from Chase, and the over-55s are not prominent in the chocolate bar market. So who *is* in the market?

ABCD identified two market sectors for Chase:

1. 15–24-year-olds looking for a pleasant-tasting snack they can eat on the move.
2. 25–34-year-old mothers wanting to pack something sustaining into their schoolchildren's lunch-boxes.

A small research project was undertaken to find out what qualities these two groups looked for in a chocolate bar, and how Chase rated against its competitors. This is how the two groups assessed *qualities*:

Desirable qualities of chocolate bars

Quality	Group 1: 15–24-year-olds think 'important' (%)	Group 2: 25–34-year-old mothers think 'important' (%)
Sustaining	38	46
Quick energy	52	29
Calorie count	43	26
Fun to eat	32	29
Easy to eat	65	35
Price	25	49

'Rating against competitors' was tested in two ways. One group from each of the target areas was shown wrappers of the competing products and asked to comment on the qualities mentioned above; another group in each case was given samples of the actual products. Here is a summary of the findings:

Chase was rated second on 'price' and 'easy to eat' by Group 1.

Chase was rated second on 'sustaining' by Group 2.

Chase scored consistently higher in the sample tests than on the wrappers on 'sustaining' and 'quick energy'.

From this, ABCD concluded that Chase needed better presentation, and should concentrate on its 'sustaining' and 'quick energy' qualities, with some emphasis also on its being 'easy to eat'.

Armed with these findings, ABCD now prepared its campaign strategy.

Taplow's Hardware

Robert Taplow, you will remember, had decided that what his shops could offer better than the large DIY stores was advice and service. In this way he hoped to expand from the shops' existing market of older people, without cars, buying occasionally in small quantities and doing small DIY jobs.

But who were the people who would be the new customers? Robert thought back to his visits to the out-of-town stores. Housewives, certainly. It was obvious that a lot of housewives were doing the decorating, but it seemed quite likely that they were not very knowledgeable if they came across some unexpected problem like damp patches or stains. Then there were the weekend decorators, the Thrapsley and district commuters. They'd probably welcome a few hints on how to do the job. Having identified these two groups as a start, Robert called on a friend of his in the town who ran a firm called Y and Z Publicity.

A large element in research is observation and accurate interpretation. The ABCD agency, proposing to spend a good deal of Chase money, needed to go further and justify their conclusions with hard research; but it may well be that they would have reached the same findings anyway. Taplow's were not planning to spend a great deal, and in any case no research was needed (other than Robert's subjective kind) to identify the problem and a possible solution.

Beaver Generators

The company's life having been spent mainly in general engineering, Beaver were faced with the problem of investigating an entirely new market. Their need was for something closer to intelligence-gathering than to market research. Who, for example, was responsible among computer users for choosing and buying capital equipment? Who were the decision-takers? How much control did the computer staff have? Who were the people who mattered? How could Beaver get their message to the key personnel?

Beaver's local marketing consultants recommended calling in the services of a specialist consultancy to answer these questions. Beavers's anonymity was to be preserved at this stage, in order to protect them from competitors, and the report commissioned from the computer specialists was wider-ranging than was strictly necessary for Beaver's needs, so that the reason for the inquiries could not be closely identified. From the specialists' report, the local consultants selected the information relevant to Beaver and presented it in an edited version. Three main points emerged:

1. Beaver's market consisted of a few hundred key people who could be reached by direct mail.
2. There were two periodicals widely read by the target group.
3. Beaver's presence at the major trade exhibition in the field would establish their credibility among potential buyers.

It was agreed that Beaver's consultants would draw up a co-ordinated plan based on activity in these three areas.

7 The agency

No one knows how many advertising agencies there are in Britain, but some estimates put the number as high as 1000. If this is correct, some of them, probably most, must be doing very small business indeed. What is known is that the agencies' trade organization, the Institute of Practitioners in Advertising, has about 270 members and commands somewhere between 85 per cent and 95 per cent of all advertising expenditure placed by UK agencies. But even within this 270 there is a great deal of diversity. The agencies whose names are known even outside the advertising world, such as J. Walter Thompson and Saatchi and Saatchi, each employ several hundred people and had turnovers – 'billings' to the trade – in 1984 approaching, or more than, £150 million each. The top 25 agencies reported billings for 1984 of over £40 million; it is among these that are to be found most of the large, big-spending consumer clients such as Procter & Gamble, Mars, Kellogg's, Imperial Tobacco and Rowntree Mackintosh. The top 25 are also the agencies most likely to be featured in front-page news stories in *Campaign*, since the shift of one client, or a single client's product, from one agency to another can significantly change the pecking order in the advertising business as a whole, to say nothing of the redundancies it can cause. The moves between these top agencies, accompanied as they are by shouts of joy and moans of grief, largely account for advertising's reputation as a volatile, temperamental business – as indeed it is at this rarefied level. But this is to ignore the fact that there are hundreds of smaller agencies doing sterling if less noisy work for clients who are well satisfied and remain with their agents for years.

The Guinness story

All the same, it is worth looking at the recent history of one national brand name, which illustrates the pleasures and pains in the top echelons of the agency business. Since the 1930s, with the toucan and the rest of the Guinness menagerie, Guinness has been a prominent and insistent advertiser which had, until 1982, used only two agencies: first Bensons, later absorbed into Ogilvy and Mather, and then J. Walter Thompson. In 1981, a new chairman was appointed, who faced the challenge of restoring the fortunes of a company that, both in sales terms and in stock market appeal, had lost its former lustre. The sales fact was a simple one: the increased popularity of lager (including Guinness's own Harp brand) had cut Guinness's market share in half.

J. Walter Thompson's successors were Allen Brady and Marsh, who came up after a year's research with the 'Friends of the Guinnless' concept, based on the idea of a 'Recovery Service' which rushed supplies of the dark-brown liquid to those in need. Expenditure on this campaign in all its variants was, in 1983, £9·5 million, almost all of it on television, and took Allen Brady and Marsh to fifth place in the 'Top Twenty' agencies. But it soon became clear that all was not well with the 'Guinnless' campaign, despite an increase in volume sales of stout. In the autumn of 1984, Guinness announced that the account was again up for grabs.

The news electrified the advertising world. It was felt that Allen Brady and Marsh had not been given enough of a chance, but this sympathetic thought was tempered by the reflection that ABM's loss would be someone else's great gain. Every agency with any reputation at all, and several with none, put in a bid. The eventual winner, via a provisional short-list of ten and a final short-list of three, was Ogilvy and Mather, with the 'Genius' theme that broke upon Britain's TV screens in the summer of 1985. The choice sent Allen Brady and Marsh spinning down from fifth to thirteenth place in the 'Top Twenty'.

But it would be wrong to make too much of circus shows like the Guinness saga. While it illustrates that a company's awareness of its advertising increases sharply when sales are in trouble and that the possibility of grabbing a large account can send agencies into paroxysms of activity, the fact is that changes of accounts between agencies represent only between 5 and 8 per cent of total advertising expenditure each year – and only some of these, of course, are big spenders. At the same time, there are agency/client relationships, such as that between J. Walter Thompson and Kellogg's, that have lasted for more than half a century.

Little and large

Because advertising agencies vary so enormously in size, and because they owe their identity to the personalities who are their guiding lights, no two are the same in the way they work or in their structure. There are some which specialize in industrial or financial advertising, some which handle very little media advertising but produce sales literature and other 'below the line' items, others which do little more than book space for ads which the advertiser supplies. Those in the last category, though usually among the smallest agencies, are in fact closest to the origins of the agency system.

The growth of the press media in the nineteenth century, which created the climate in which the advertising business began to grow, also created a problem for media owners: how to exploit the value of their advertising space among thousands of potential advertisers? The answer that emerged was the advertising agency in its original form. The first agencies were the media's rather than the clients', selling space to advertisers on commission. These simple beginnings are still reflected in the way agencies are usually paid; this is by commission on sales of space and time. The commission varies from 15 per cent, or occasionally more, for the consumer media – that is, the popular press, radio and television – to as little as 5 per cent from some trade publications. By logical extension, the agencies also collect commission on the costs of production such as film, artwork, typesetting and so on. In practice, the agencies 'buy' space, time or services from the media or supplier at a preferential rate and 'sell' them to the client at the full rate.

The commission system is, however, no longer universal. For a number of reasons, agents and clients may prefer to work on a fee basis. For example, an agency that provides the client with what amounts to a full marketing consultancy, as many do, will expect to pick up more than the odd bit of commission from the media. An agency may find itself involved in the re-formulation or re-packaging of a product (as the ABCD agency does, as we shall see, with Chase) and this work will attract an agreed fee, in addition to the commission earned from the media. There is an infinite number of variations between commission only and fee only, dictated by the nature of the agency's role, the amount (and type) of media advertising involved, and the negotiating skills of agency and client. With some TV spots costing well over £12 500 for one 30-second spot in one ITV area, an agency handling a substantial TV campaign is obviously going to make more out of commission than one handling a campaign in the trade press.

Virtually all agencies, however, have one problem in common: regulating the work-flow. Among the larger agencies, the acquisition of a demanding new client can cause almost as much disturbance as the loss of a profitable old one; for this reason, agencies sometimes turn down offers to pitch for new business even when they have been specifically invited to do so. The news of a prestigious new account spreads quickly, and can easily make existing clients suspect that they will not be getting so much of the agency's time and top talent in future; naturally enough, they resent any suggestion that they are being palmed off with the 'second eleven'. To avoid this, expansionist agencies have to do something of a juggling act to keep *all* the clients in the spotlight *all* the time. The strain of doing this is one of the reasons for the splits, mergers and new partnerships which are such a feature of the advertising business at its top levels.

At the other end of the scale, smaller agencies make extensive use of outside services and freelances to even out the flow of work – though this too can have disadvantages in terms of client relations. Clients tend to expect agencies to have enough confidence in their talent to employ it full-time. In specialized and technical fields, however, it clearly makes sense to use outside talent on accounts which are not big enough to justify in-house employees.

The agency structure

Agency operations can be broken down into a number of departments, though department names and precise functions vary from one agency to another, while in the smaller ones some functions are farmed out to suppliers.

Put simply, the agency's job is to:

> identify the advertiser's needs;
>
> suggest ways of satisfying those needs;
>
> carry out or commission any necessary research;
>
> buy appropriate space or time;
>
> arrange for the production of advertisements;
>
> deliver the finished advertisements to the appropriate media;
>
> carry out or commission any follow-up research;
>
> in consultation with the media specialists, to draw up a media policy – that is, the balance of media to be used;
>
> to follow through detailed planning with the client.

The creative team consists basically of a copywriter and an art director; in a large agency, there will be many creative teams working more or less independently. The two functions, writing and art, are not as distinct as the previous sentence might suggest: essentially, the creative team consists of two people who can work creatively together, strike sparks off each other and yet take each other's criticism. Smaller agencies sometimes buy in their creative talent from outside, and in that case will probably go to some lengths to keep the client and the creative team apart.

The creative team 'thinks up the ads'. Working to a creative brief provided by the account executive, writer and art director play with ideas until the shape of something good begins to emerge. This will not necessarily – or, in the case of a large consumer account, usually – be one idea. When Allen Brady and Marsh were working on the Guinness account, they developed and tested no fewer than seven separate campaigns before deciding on the winner. This was unusual, however; perhaps even excessive. More commonly, a handful of ideas is discussed with the agency's creative head, and perhaps three or four of these are roughed out to show to the client. If the agency is pitching for new business, the selected ideas will be worked up into finished artwork in the case of press ads, or an 'animatic' (a kind of proof commercial using drawings or photographs) in the case of TV. Normally, however, the client will first see the creative team's ideas as 'roughs' (outline drawings with the headline drawn in felt-pen) or 'storyboards' (successions of drawings or photographs showing the outlines of the commercials' 'stories').

Account management provides the contact at senior level between agency and client. The agency's team is led by an account executive or sometimes by the account director, which may or may not mean that he is a director of the agency itself. The account executive, perhaps aided by an assistant, normally chairs contact meetings and presents the agency's proposals, though members of the creative team or other specialists – in market research, for example – may be called upon to present their particular sectors of the proposals. Although the account executive is the 'agency's man' (or woman), he is expected to understand the client's business, aims and preoccupations in some depth, and he is to some extent the buffer between the ideas of the agency and the objectives of the client. Obviously, this demands considerable experience of both advertising and the business world, and account executives have often spent some part of their previous career on the other side of the table, as part of a client company's marketing team. Above all, the account executive must be able to see outside the world of advertising. The effects of an advertising campaign may spill over into any number of industrial problems – production difficulties, labour relations, the distribution network – and the anticipation of these may weigh heavily with the client's representatives as they hear the agency's proposals. Account management is a field for fast thinkers, diplomats and people with an instinctive understanding of other people's problems.

The functions of the account team are:

> to develop a marketing strategy on which the advertising campaign will be based;

> to define the strategic aims and the target audience;

in consultation with the creative team, to draw up the creative strategy.

When the client's approval of one of the ideas has been obtained, it may – still in its rough form – be 'pre-tested' with a group of typical consumers. 'Pre-testing' is a form of research full of subtleties. Most people outside the advertising business rate television commercials, if they rate them at all, on their entertainment value. It is nice for a manufacturer to feel that he is providing some entertainment to potential consumers, but that is not the point of advertising. 'Pre-testing' aims to find out, not what the viewer thinks of the commercial, but what images he retains and what messages come across. To take an extreme example of this, no TV commercial would ever show someone having indigestion, going down to the chemist's, asking his advice, and coming home with the client's product. This would give the viewer quite the wrong idea: that *if* you get indigestion, you can get something for it from the chemist. What makers of indigestion remedies want to get across is that *when* you have indigestion, you can take some of their products which you have prudently bought in advance and put in the medicine cupboard. The difference between the two messages, in sales terms, is of course enormous. 'Wrong' messages can come across – and be revealed in pre-testing – in all sorts of ways.

Assuming that the proposed ads score well in pre-testing, the next stage is for the creative team to start putting together the finished artwork or commercial. The writer produces (in the case of a press ad) his 'body copy' – the text below the headline. The art director commissions, through the art buyer in the case of a large agency or directly in a smaller one, photography or illustrations. The scripts of radio or television commercials are prepared. And the whole lot is presented to the client for final approval. The art director will closely oversee, to the extent of being present at photo sessions and even looking over a typesetter's shoulder, everything that has to do with the appearance of the ad. When TV shooting begins, both members of the creative team will be on hand, selecting the shots to be used, if necessary altering the script as shooting goes along, approving (or not, as the case may be) the rushes of each day's work.

A large agency will have a number of sections in its creative departments which provide services to the creative team: for example, an art studio, a typographer, and a section which specializes in liaison with television production companies and involves itself in such matters as the casting and direction of commercials.

The media department is responsible for advising on the choice of media for a particular campaign and for buying space or time. In the larger agencies, *media planning* is differentiated from *media buying*, though practice varies according to the prejudices of the agency directors. What is certain is that both functions demand an intimate knowledge of the media, their audiences, and their own plans.

A given amount of money can buy X, Y or Z exposures of an advertisement, whether in print or on the air. In advertising language, the budget buys a number of OTS – opportunities to see. The job of the media planner is to get the maximum OTS in the target audience for the advertiser's money. Not all media are equal in pulling power as far as advertising is concerned, and it is the media planner's job to know which of a range of equivalent publications is likely to be most effective, which TV stations, and so on. The media buyer is at heart a figures man, skilled in negotiating off the cuff, quick to pick up details of any discounts or other special offers – such as help with merchandising – being offered by media as a 'come-on', and adept at playing off, for example, the advantages of predetermined TV slots against those of a package offering a number of Guaranteed Housewife Impressions. The trickiest part of the whole media operation, especially if different types of media are involved, is constructing the schedule so that the whole thing comes together in the way that the client expects.

Traffic. At the height of preparation for a single advertising campaign for a single client, there are perhaps hundreds of items moving between suppliers and the agency, within the agency, from the agency to other suppliers or finishers, and between the agency and the client. Take the simple example of a photograph which is to be used in a press ad for scent. The photographer will have to be commissioned and briefed, in writing as well as face to face. After the photo session, he sends in his contacts. These are passed round the agency – from art director to creative head, from creative head to account executive and back again – and several full-size prints are ordered. When these arrive, they are again passed round, and the final selection made for showing to the client. The approved print goes back to the studio to be printed again, perhaps re-touched ready for the press. If the intended space for the ad is in a periodical printed by letterpress (though in fact it is unlikely to be, in the case of an ad for scent), the print has to be made into a block at a block-maker's. All in all, this one image, in its various forms, will have made several journeys to and from the agency and a similar number inside it; and all these journeys will have to be made within a finite time, to meet the printing deadline.

This process is replicated with illustrations, small pieces of art-work, typesetting, proofs, rough and fine cuts of film, all of which have to be received, dealt with and despatched at the due time. It is small wonder that the traffic department (sometimes called progress, control or production) is often regarded as the key to a successful agency. No matter how brilliant the ideas produced by the creative team or how skilful the media planners and buyers may be, the whole thing will fall down unless the various elements are kept moving. Traffic is progress-chasing *plus* meticulous record-keeping, so that the stage reached by any particular operation can be pin-pointed, *plus*, at times, the skills needed to persuade a supplier to come in over the weekend to do a vital piece of typesetting or print developing, preferably at no extra cost.

The service departments.   As has already been indicated, agencies vary in the extent to which they have their own in-house services. It is possible to run an effective agency with an account department, a creative team and a media department alone, or even without the third of these, or even with all three functions telescoped under the control of a couple of people. Many agencies work this way not because they can't afford better resources but from choice, believing that small is most effective.

Among the most common service departments to be found in the larger agencies, however, are:

Print and production. This department separates out the progress-chasing functions of the media department and also deals with basic proof-reading, marking up artwork for size and the other routine jobs connected with getting an advertisement into print.

TV production. TV production departments do the equivalent job to print and production. They do not, in fact, produce commercials, which are made by outside companies, but they help select actors or personalities, directors, designers and so on. They may also have a traffic function in terms of pre-production (building sets, rehearsals and so on), post-production (adding sound, editing, final editing), and distribution of the finished commercials to the TV programme companies.

Research. Some agencies have their own research departments, which act as 'research traffic' departments rather than carrying out detailed work themselves. The research department can include the library and other information services.

Running an agency

An advertising agency, like any other business, has to be managed. It is not always easy to discern, from an agency's letterhead or even from more detailed information, which directors are the actual managers and which have courtesy titles designed to establish their standing with clients. Somewhere, however, there will be a financial director, because good financial management is vital not only in the usual way, for the viability of the business, but because agencies depend on their good standing with the media they use. The agency business is a peculiar one in two ways. First, it is a business with an extremely high 'value added' content. The raw materials involved in creating advertising are negligible, but the costs in terms of skills are high. Secondly, agencies are liable for large sums of money which they owe to the media and which will only come back to them, plus commission, when the client pays his bills. This is a situation which is all too vulnerable unless cash-flow is carefully controlled, and even the mundane billing operation is carried out with the utmost skill and care. The media themselves – who of course would stand to lose substantially if an agency failed – are keenly alive to the financial soundness of agencies, and are in a position, if they choose, to turn down bookings or ask for some kind of guarantee.

The huge amounts of money in circulation between agencies, the media and clients – in 1983, the top ten advertisers spent well over £500 million – explain one of the factors behind the recent trend for the larger agencies to become public limited companies.

Advertising without an agency

It is, of course, quite possible to be an advertiser without using an agent, and many companies, including some large ones, are. It may well make sense for a group of companies spending a good deal of money advertising a large number of products to have its own in-house agency service; this indeed was what Unilever – as a group, still Britain's largest advertiser – did for many years until it sold its Lintas agency. If one looks a little more closely, however, the idea becomes less attractive. A group of sufficient size to make it worth while is likely to have products spread across a wide range of markets; even a company like Natwest with one basic product – banking – will want to advertise to a number of different audiences; students, businessmen looking for overdrafts, and people saving for their old age, for example. The skills necessary to do an effective job in all these areas are probably better sought on the open market, among the advertising agencies, than under a company's own roof. There is, too, a value to be placed on the expertise of people who are not 'company men', who can bring a fresh view to a company's problems, and whose position is independent enough to tell a client, if necessary, that his product is rubbish. (And in case this sounds unlikely, agencies do, in fact, sometimes turn down clients whose products they don't like. One of the leading London agencies, for example, will not handle cigarette advertising.)

The 'fresh view' argument applies to any company tempted to put its advertising in the hands of a marketing department. The inside eye may simply not see clearly enough. One marketing man recalls a period when he worked for a manufacturer of simulated-leather furnishings made of plastics. In the light of a rash of public concern about the fire hazards of plastic coverings, the company's advertising

– run in-house – made much of the extensive testing and proven safety of the product. Within the company, this had become a very important issue, perhaps obscuring all others. But the new, safe covering refused to take off in the market, and an agency was called in. On a visit to the factory, one of the agency people noticed straight away what made this manufacturer's product different from others in the field: when you sat down on it or moved about on it, it didn't make embarrassing noises like a joke cushion. Overwhelmed by test data from the technical department, the company's own marketing team had failed to observe, or perhaps failed to place any value on, this simple fact. Promoted with a series of ads using a 'Sitting Quietly?' line, the product was soon reaching its sales targets. The consumer, it seemed, was less concerned about fire safety than about making unsocial noises.

Another hazard about doing it yourself is that too many people think they know about advertising and can produce an effective advertisement, just as too many people think, without the slightest justification, they can write or paint or sing. You have only to see a selection of amateur efforts at creating advertisements to discover how fallacious this is. Some people really do believe that a picture of a large loaf with the legend 'Buy Bloggs' Bread' is going to lead to a riot at the baker's. Others (and, it must be admitted, not all of these are amateurs) cheerfully lift lines from other people's ads ('. . . the parts other . . . cannot reach', 'Probably the best . . . in the world') in complete confidence that what has sold lager can equally well sell, say, machine tools. Others again believe that the line (or, as they would say, the slogan) is all, and can hardly contain their excitement at having strung three or four words together. Prominent advertisers are plagued by letters (and, even worse, examples) from people who think they have just the right ad to seal the company's future. They completely ignore the fact that, even if their efforts showed talent, the creative element in advertising is only the visible one-ninth of the iceberg in terms of the skills of all kinds that go into a successful campaign.

Probably the only advertiser outside the big league who should go it alone is the one whose media spend is so small that no agency is interested in the business. Such an advertiser is likely to be in the professional or specialized industrial market, with a strictly limited number of potential customers. Even so, he may well need some help with sales or technical literature, and looking after advertising could be part of the deal for an outside agency – not necessarily primarily an *advertising* agency – dealing with this.

There is, however, a half-way house between using a full agency service and doing it yourself, and the signs are that this intermediate process will become more common. Much the same is beginning to happen in advertising as happened a decade or more ago in printing. In the old days, if you wanted something printed you took your copy and pictures along to a printer and left it to him to do the lot. Now, the collection of processes that go into the production of print is increasingly broken down: someone does the typesetting, a chap round the corner pastes it up into artwork, there's a little place down the road where the plates are made, and the 'printer', new style, is simply the owner of printing machinery. Advertising has not yet become as fragmented as that, but the early signs are there, most noticeably with the separation out of the media function.

'Media independents' specializing in media buying are a fairly recent import from the United States. Fiercely opposed at first by the traditional agencies who (rightly) saw in this development the seeds of the collapse of the time-honoured commission system, the media shops have now become accepted as a legitimate part of the business. Parallel with this, there has been a growth in fee-paid creative consultancies which carry out only the account management and creative functions. This arrangement has the merit of setting people to do what they can do best, and it has also enabled bright creative people to set up shop without having to find the financial backing to satisfy the media, since the media independents have taken on the role of debtors.

The agency and the client

The relationship between an advertising agency and its client has been likened, in the extravagant way advertising people have of inflating their self-image, to marriage. This may be fanciful, but it is certainly true that advertising and wedlock share certain characteristics, including the need for understanding, sympathy and sensitivity on both sides, if they are to work. Agency and client do not stand in the same relation to each other as supplier and customer.

Where the agency is to be paid by commission from the media, this may be true in strictly practical terms. But the subtleties of the agency/client relationship go beyond that. In the first place, the agency is going to get an insight into the most confidential aspects of the client's business otherwise vouchsafed only to accountants and auditors, and probably into the details of internal company politics that never show up on balance sheets. This implies that there must be trust on both sides: the client must trust the agency with its commercial secrets, while the agency, if it is to do a proper job on the account, must feel that it is being given access to all the necessary information.

Advertising is fond of saying that it is a 'people business', and this is of course true. The people from both agency and client company who are going to deal with each other in the course of a campaign must feel that the others are people they can do business with. An agency pitching for a new account will have done its homework on the potential client and will aim its pitch at what it hopes is the right level. If it makes a mistake at this stage, things are unlikely to improve; personality clashes are reckoned to be the prime reason for the failure of pitches for new business, as well as for subsequent partings of the ways.

Major clients looking for a new agency normally short-list three or four. These are invited to meet the client's key personnel who will be involved in the proposed campaign, and given a briefing session. In addition, a written brief is supplied to the agency, which is then asked to prepare a presentation. At the big-money end of the business, with the most extrovert agencies, the presentation can be a real showbiz affair, with jingles, dancing-girls and all. More usually, it is an office meeting between the principals on both sides. At this stage, no one expects a complete campaign plan to be revealed; the object of a presentation is not to sell ideas but to sell the agency as the most likely source of good ideas. (Exceptionally, when Ogilvy and Mather won the Guinness account in 1984, they did so at their presentation by unveiling the 'Genius' concept which, in effect, became the campaign. But this was an unusual occasion not only in this respect but also because Ogilvy and Mather's men were told straight away that they had won.)

Some larger agencies go to some lengths to keep their creative people away from the clients, leaving it to the account team to carry on the face-to-face work. It is probably true to say that clients prefer to be able to talk to the people who are actually working on the ads, and there is, of course, some risk in second-hand communications. What certainly disturbs clients greatly is if, during the course of a series of meetings, they see too many different faces, especially if the faces tend to look progressively more junior. While it is likely that the senior agency people at the presentation will not be those the client will meet on a day-to-day basis, it is important that, once agency and client are doing business, the client gets a feeling of commitment and stability.

Keeping the relationship sweet

Something that disturbs many agency/client relationships is the sense on the part of the client that the agency is only just managing to keep the ball in the air. Some advertising people cultivate a 'hectic' image; others have it thrust upon them because it is a fact of life that the most carefully prepared schedule often turns out to be too tight. However, it is a mistake to think that all clients accept hasty phone-calls and quick turn-round times as a necessary part of the advertising business; many dislike the feeling that the tail is wagging the dog. Whatever crises are raging in the agency's offices, the noise should be confined there. A good traffic department will have anticipated any problems. Of course, things sometimes go wrong; messengers are delayed, printers miss their deadlines, machines break down. But an efficient agency keeps these problems, as far as possible, to itself.

But clients, too, have their obligations in keeping the relationship sweet. Those with large marketing departments, used to handling deadlines, are likely to respect schedules; people with little experience of print and the media generally, however, often fail to appreciate how important timetables are. A common complaint about smaller advertisers is that they sometimes fail to see what problems are caused by last-minute changes in copy, for example. One advertising man has bitter memories of an ad that had been approved all the way through until the client's marketing manager thought to show a final proof as a courtesy to his managing director. The result was a drastic change in the copy, a weekend of work in the agency, and a 400-mile round trip starting before dawn on the Monday morning to obtain approval of the revised version – which, in the agency's view, had been seriously devalued by the managing director's intervention.

8 The message

Once the target audience for an advertising campaign has been identified, the next task is to devise a message, or series of messages, that
will appeal to the market. The number of variations in style and
treatment is infinite. The approach may be cajoling, flattering, amus-
ing, merely informative, perhaps even frightening. The message may
be direct – as in a typical TV commercial for washing powder – or
oblique, as in the neo-surrealist Benson & Hedges magazine and
poster ads. The sell may be hard – as with the ranting furniture-store
managers seen on television at sale time – or appropriately soft, as
with the playful puppy in the Andrex toilet-roll commercials.

Message and treatment form part of the *advertising* strategy, which
is itself part of the overall *marketing* strategy for the brand. Advertising is only one element in the complete marketing 'mix', which
also includes such things as packaging, sales literature, the sales
mechanism and so on. While the aim of the marketing strategy may
be, say, to increase sales by 5 per cent per year for the next three
years, the advertising strategy must be more precisely targeted.
Advertising cannot be expected to shoulder the entire burden. To
take a simple case, whether or not sales increase by 5 per cent per
year depends as much on distribution and merchandising as on
advertising. The most memorable advertising campaign imaginable
will be ineffective unless, when consumers try to buy the brand,
they can find it easily in the shops. Since, in today's shops, it is
increasingly hard to find an assistant who even knows what is in
stock and where – to say nothing of one with real product knowledge
– the 'front line' activities of the marketing team have become even
more vital, and this accounts for the increase in merchandising at
the retail level to ensure that stock is displayed, and often that there
is someone with product knowledge on hand. (You didn't think
those department store 'beauty consultants' were there merely as a

free service, did you?) Merchandising and display fulfil the desire to purchase which has been stimulated by advertising, and the two elements – like the other elements in the marketing mix – are interdependent. The function of advertising is to stimulate a desire to purchase in the target audience.

An advertiser may be launching an entirely new product (for example, Yorkie, described in Chapter 1), or re-positioning an established one (for example, Chase), or fighting hard against the competition (see any lager commercial), or simply maintaining his position in the marketplace (Fairy Liquid). In each of these cases, the significance of advertising in the total marketing mix will be different, and so will the advertising treatment. The advertisements for a new hair shampoo will have to indicate what it is for; and this might be done by showing, say, a girl with a dry scalp problem 'before' and 'after' – a typical demonstration ad. Re-positioning a brand will involve justifying it to its intended new market. A highly competitive ad will point up the superiority (in quality, style, price) of the brand concerned. In maintaining a position, it is possible to be more laid-back, perhaps even self-indulgent; which is perhaps why the washing-up brand leader, Fairy Liquid, has not altered its basic 'Hands that do dishes' story-line for over twenty years.

All these considerations are taken into account in arriving at an advertising strategy. There is no point in spending money on advertising unless you know:

> what you want to say
>
> who you want to say it to
>
> what you hope to achieve.

The advertising strategy provides answers to these three questions, which are as relevant for the small business as for the large public company. In turn, the answers dictate the form of the message. The relationship between strategy and message can be seen in the following examples of two well-remembered campaigns.

Campari goes downmarket

In the mid-1970s Findlater Matta, the UK concessionaires for Campari, had a problem. Campari had been around for a century or more, but in the mid-1960s it had become widely accepted as a sophisticated drink, with soda, in the upwardly mobile sector of the middle classes. By 1975, however, this marketing pitch had become self-limiting: Campari drinkers were getting older, their income had been hit by inflation, and expense-account drinking, which had partly accounted for Campari's success, was under pressure from recession. There was a clear need to broaden Campari's appeal, extending it to younger, downmarket drinkers.

The result was a series of television commercials featuring the then unknown cockney girl, Lorraine Chase. The running theme of the series was the confrontation between a traditional middle-class Campari-and-soda drinker and the coarse-vowelled Lorraine, who was drinking Campari and lemonade. *What the ads said* was that some people liked Campari and soda, but Campari went with lemonade, too; that Campari wasn't only for 'toffs' who liked their drinks bitter but also for 'people like you'. The 'people like you' – the answer to the second question – were young C1 and C2 drinkers who were used to sweeter tastes than Campari's. The achievements at which the campaign was aimed were to appeal to a new market of younger drinkers, and to break the inevitability of the Campari-and-soda link. At the same time, Campari did not want to alienate the established 'with soda' market, so there was a certain amount of tightrope-walking in the campaign.

Specifically, Campari wanted the target audience to become aware of the drink, and to try it; and the success or otherwise of the campaign was checked at intervals by research into 'awareness and trial'. These showed that, for example, whereas in 1975 (before the campaign) 66 per cent of all adults were aware of Campari and 20 per cent had tried it, by 1979 (three years into the campaign) 82 per cent were aware, and 30 per cent had tasted. Further research into the age of the tasters revealed that more younger people (47 per cent of 15–34-year-olds in 1979, against 35 per cent in 1975) were trying Campari.

Over the period of the Lorraine Chase commercials, 1976–80 (and, of course, of other supporting activities in the marketing area), volume sales of Campari increased by 62 per cent, outstripping the growth in sales of vodka, vermouth, whisky or gin.

Barclaycard answers doubt

Like other bank credit cards, Barclaycard derives its income from two sources: from a percentage paid by retailers who accept the card against purchases, and from interest charged on Barclaycard holders who do not settle their account in full within the period allowed. Unlike its main credit-card rival, Access, Barclaycard also functions as a cheque guarantee card, but its use in this way of course brings no financial benefit to the company. Unlike charge cards such as Diners Club and American Express (which require settlement in full each month), bank credit cards are supplied and replaced free; there is no joining fee and no annual subscription. So unless Barclaycard is used as a *credit* card it is merely a convenient facility provided at the company's expense.

Research in the mid-1970s showed that one Barclaycard holder in three only rarely used his or her card to obtain credit, and then usually only in an emergency. These holders perceived the card as primarily for guaranteeing cheques. Typical reasons given were the fear of getting into debt, a lingering resistance to the idea of credit on moral grounds, and failure to understand the system, especially the fact that no interest was incurred if monthly statements were paid in full on time. The aim of a new advertising campaign which started in 1977 was to overcome these objections to the greater use of Barclaycard in its credit function, and in particular to reassure holders who feared that they would be carried away to excess if they used the card to buy on credit. It was hoped also to convert the large number of people who refused to own a Barclaycard at all, for fear of falling into temptation.

The chosen medium was the Sunday colour supplements, and the strategy was to state the objections to Barclaycard credit and then produce reassuring arguments against them. For example, one graphic ad showed a man turning back his jacket front to reveal his Barclaycard burning a hole in his inside pocket, a perfect representation of one of the nightmares expressed in the research. On the contrary, the copy argued: using Barclaycard can actually save you money, by avoiding the need for a bank overdraft, enabling you to snap up a bargain when you see one, or spreading the cost of an annual season ticket.

At the beginning of the campaign Barclaycard holders were, typically, 25–44-year-old-men in the higher social grades living in the Midlands and South of England. Barclaycard, in its campaign, wanted to talk to these people (to persuade them to use their cards more for credit purchases) and to other credit-worthy people (to persuade them to become cardholders). What Barclaycard wanted to say was that, far from being a danger, credit cards were a help to 'people like them'. What it was hoped to achieve was a change in attitude towards the use of credit cards, and increased use among existing holders of the Barclaycard for credit purposes. Regular attitude research, together with data from within the Barclaycard organization, confirmed that the objectives were being achieved – and indeed, in due course, in the early 1980s, Barclaycard was able to announce the doubling of the 1977 number of cardholders.

The tools of the trade

So the advertiser has decided on his advertising strategy, on the message he wants to get across, who he wants to receive it, and what results he expects. Now he, together with his agency if he has one, must consider ways and means. He has at his disposal a variety of approaches, some of which were mentioned at the beginning of this chapter. He also has the tools of advertising – the elements that make up the individual advertisements. It is time to consider these in detail.

Television

Essentially, of course, television consists of pictures plus sound (in that order), but the visual and the aural can be broken down into further categories. The visual can vary from a simple 'pack-shot' (a picture of, say, a packet of breakfast cereal), through a demonstration (perhaps of the effect of a new shampoo on dry hair), to a dramatic 'playlet' (in which, for example, the advertised brand plays a part in a potted boy-meets-girl story). The sound-track might be orchestral music, a specially composed jingle, an established popular song (normally 'popular' rather than 'pop' because of copyright considerations), sound effects on their own, dialogue for a playlet, straight-to-camera speech with the speaker in vision, a voiceover (the voice of an unseen speaker) or any combination of these. Among all these variations, the simplest spots are those that appear as run-of-programme fillers on regional stations and consist merely of a still slide with a voiceover read by a continuity announcer. At the other extreme are the more memorable and expensive playlets using well-known names and faces, such as the Leonard Rossiter/Joan Collins series for Cinzano and the 1985 British Gas campaign which found Colin Welland in a variety of suitable locales (a theme also used simultaneously in magazine advertising).

The most important thing about a TV commercial, however much or little it costs to produce, is that it is first and foremost visual. Even a single still picture can be visually stimulating, and there is really no need for the imagination to stop short (as it does distressingly often in regional still-and-voiceover slots) at a picture of the advertiser's shop-front. However, almost every night it is possible to see more ambitious commercials whose producers have forgotten the simple rule that, in television, pictures come first. On the other hand, just as common is the commercial whose stunning visuals you admire and remember, without remembering what they were advertising. The art of the commercial producer is to steer steadily between the twin hazards of unmemorability, and memorability for the wrong reason.

The other two elements available in a television commercial, in addition to picture quality, are colour and movement. How these are used depends to some extent on the nature of the product and also on the grammar of television. For example, quick cutting was in vogue in the early 1980s, and was used successfully for a range of products stretching from cornflakes to sunglasses; but it would probably not be suitable for scent or boxes of chocolates, which tend towards a more dreamy, romantic image. (Though it may be, of course, that by the time this book appears someone will have proved that sentence wrong.) It has to be remembered, too, that the visuals must be appropriate to the target audience; it may be tempting to toy with the colour possibilities of disco-style lighting, but it happens that this particular sector of popular culture is known to, and appreciated by, the sector of the population which views television least.

A problem faced by all television advertisers is that their commercials, in order to achieve the required penetration, have to be repeated several times a day over several weeks. Some viewers will come to know them by heart. A commercial which may look fine on first appearance may well begin to pall. This makes humour a difficult thing to handle on TV. However good the joke is, it may not last the campaign. The Leonard Rossiter/Joan Collins series of commercials for Cinzano were such a success because of the perfection of Rossiter's timing, which was of such a calibre that it could be watched with delight time and time again. For my money, the much-lamented PG chimps were in the same league, though the timing here was not that of the performers but of the cutters and dubbers. When humour fails, however, it tends to do so disastrously. What people do when the commercials are showing – leave the room, zap to another channel, fill in their pools coupons – is enough of a problem without positively inviting them to switch off.

A little-considered aspect of TV commercials, perhaps because agencies and clients see them in optimum conditions in viewing theatres, is what happens in the last frame. Because of the problems associated with the timing of commercial breaks, it often happens that the last frame of the last commercial in a sequence remains frozen on the screen until the television station rejoins the network. If this happens to be a pack-shot, the advertiser gets a bonus of extra exposure for nothing; but if it is the last frame of a playlet with what was intended to be a crisp ending, the effect can be, to say the least, unfortunate. Moving pictures are not intended to be seen as stills (film and TV publicity stills are always shot separately, *as* stills) and a persisting image of, say, someone with his mouth half-open in astonishment may not be the best sign-off for a commercial. No doubt this is something that regional presentation staff should do something about, but the fact remains that they tend not to since, in the absence of anything to fill, television abhors an empty screen. It is always as well to remember that the viewer will not be seeing the commercials in viewing theatre conditions.

Voiceovers may use a well-known personality such as Jimmy Young for washing powder, but most use voices unknown outside their rather specialized field, some of whom are 'voicealikes'. (There is a host of actors in the gravelly-voice market, all trying to sound like Orson Welles or Patrick Allen.) The choice between known and unknown voices is a subject hotly debated in the advertising world. It is argued on one side that the association of a known personality with a product enhances it, and on the other that this enhancement will be instantly debased if the well-known voice is also heard speaking for some other product, even if it is nowhere near the same product range. There is an additional problem regarding well-known names, whether in voice or on camera, in that IBA rules prohibit the inclusion of ads featuring actors in breaks within or around programmes in which the same actors are appearing.

The press message

There are five elements available to an advertiser in the press, though he may not use all of them. They are:

> the headline
>
> the body copy
>
> the visual
>
> the logo and/or pack-shot
>
> the coupon.

The headline is what should catch the reader's eye, and detain him. Usually it contains the basic message, though it can also be used as a 'come-on' to persuade the reader to read on to the body copy. Here are some examples of headlines from the week this chapter was written:

> — *Soundproof your home in seconds* (3-in-1 oil)
> — *Take good care of yourself* (Hermesetas sweeteners)
> — *These motorists cut the cost of their motor insurance – so can you!* (Direct Line Insurance, Royal Bank of Scotland)
> — *Don't wait – decorate!* (Home Charm Stores)

- *For a clear voice and a clear throat* (Imps cough pastilles)
- *The book that shook Threadneedle Street* (Abbey National Cheque-Save Account)

The headline may say it all (many ads for well-known brands consist simply of a headline and a pack-shot) or it may be an opening gambit.

The body copy takes you further into the story. *Soundproof your home in seconds*, for example, leads to the discovery not of a new magic product, as an innocent reader might expect, but to the rediscovery of a familiar domestic item – the can of oil to stop doors and windows squeaking. To find out how the pictured motorists cut the cost of their insurance, and how you could do the same, you have to read quite a lot of body copy. But it's a subject most people are interested in and prepared to read about, and motor insurance is a fairly complex product. You wouldn't want or need, by contrast, to read very much about cough pastilles. If you're troubled that way, you need only to know where you can buy them and how much they cost. In this case, the body copy tells you, in about thirty words.

In some fields of advertising, the body copy is necessarily long, either because the subject is complex (as with motor insurance) or, as in ads for loans, pension plans and the like, there are legal requirements to be considered. Advertisers are in a quandary here in an age when the received wisdom is that, because of the influence of television, people are less and less inclined to read much more than, say, 200 words at a stretch. Copywriters have to do the best they can to keep up interest. The pictures of the insurance-wise motorists mentioned earlier aim to identify with the reader to such an extent that the necessary detail is endured.

It is less easy to explain the fashion in recent years for exceptionally long body copy where it is not necessary, for example in some quality car advertising. While there are plenty of motoring buffs prepared to read extensive technical detail, as the motoring periodicals prove, on the face of it it seems unlikely that there is the same demand for the only mildly informative, soft-sell copy that practically filled the space in the recent Volvo ads created by David Abbott, something of a pioneer in this technique.

The visual may be an illustration, a photograph, a strip-cartoon, or whatever. In some kinds of advertisements, such as those for clothes or furniture, it may be the dominant element. In stores advertising, it may simply be a collection of pack-shots with prices or '3p off' flashes across them.

The visual may have a variety of functions. It may be simply to attract attention, as with the photograph of two naked girls bathing, with the legend 'These girls are wearing swimsuits' (advertising Aquasun lotion). It may demonstrate, as occurs often in double-glazing ads. Its function may be to associate a product with a particular lifestyle (a drink with the young, 'fun-loving' set, for example, or an exotic foreign location with a particular make of car). The visual may even be typographical, as with the common device used (perhaps too often) in airline advertisements where it is a list of the destinations of the airline's flights, with a headline superimposed. If the advertiser also uses television, the press visual will often reflect, or be derived from, or be related to, the TV commercials. Some visuals have an astonishingly long life, being used in various forms over many years. Esso's tiger is an example.

The logo (derived from *logogram*, a shorthand symbol) is part of the advertiser's message. It may be a registered trade mark like the Shell symbol, Dunlop's 'Flying D' or the Woolmark, or it may be a brand name, set in a type-style common to product packaging and point-of-sale material (which may also, of course, be registered as a trade mark). Some logos have become so familiar as to be almost part of the language, like ICI's 'wavy line' and Lloyds Bank's stylized black horse. These have had a central emphasis in their respective companies' advertisements for many years. Other companies do not give their logos so much limelight, and probably few people would be able to draw or describe accurately Nabisco's logo, for example, or that of the British Sugar Corporation, for all that they appear frequently in ads and on packaging.

The coupon is the most common form of direct response advertising, though readers can also be invited to write to a freepost address (which may also be used on a coupon) or dial a freefone number. Direct response advertising has two distinct purposes, and is at its most worthwhile if both are fulfilled. The aim is not only to sell the products advertised, but also to build up a list of potential future customers. The response may take the form of an order for goods, a request for sales literature or an invitation for a representative to call. In any case, those who respond can then be added to lists for a direct mail operation.

Direct response advertising is generally suitable for items of relatively high value or for subscription goods such as books, records and prints. Its great advantage is that its success can be precisely monitored, not only over a whole campaign but also as between different newspapers or periodicals, different styles of approach, and so on. (For this reason, 'keying' a coupon so that its source can be identified is essential.) Where the coupon asks the advertiser to send information or a representative, the rate at which inquiries are converted into sales can also be measured exactly.

There are various ways of dealing with the response from coupon ads, according to the advertiser's resources. Nationwide companies will often refer inquiries to local stockists, with suitable arrangements for monitoring the follow-up. A smaller advertiser may cope with the response direct, or use a mailing house.

Two other forms of direct response must be mentioned here. One is the 'reader inquiry service' offered by many periodicals, especially in the trade, technical and professional press. This takes the form of a single coupon on which the reader ticks the numbers of the advertisements in which he is interested. This is either passed on to the advertiser or dealt with centrally by the periodical's advertisement department. It is, of course, suitable only for supplying sales literature or further information.

The other, confined to retailers, invites the reader to cut out the advertisement, or part of it, and present it at the shop in exchange for a discount. It is an effective way of getting customers into a new shop, and of enabling a new business to gauge the effectiveness of the rival local media.

Radio

In Britain at least, where historically there has been little opportunity to build up a corpus of expertise, radio advertising is very much a poor relation. Writers of radio commercials are in an unenviable position: they have nothing to use but sound, and yet they need to have a good visual perception of what is happening in the script. They also have to face the unpalatable fact that their work is going to be heard (probably in less than perfect conditions) in a context of aural wallpaper.

For these reasons among others, similarities between radio and television commercials are only superficial. Radio may indeed be used to support a television campaign, using the same voices, similar dramatic situations, the same jingles; but if they do, it is well for the radio writers to realize that they are dependent on this crutch. The general rule in radio is 'Keep it simple', bearing in mind both the likely listening conditions and the fact that, in order to achieve sufficient coverage, radio commercials have a high repeat rate.

The great advantage that radio has is that the production of commercials is relatively cheap. The trick is to make sure they don't sound it. Anyone who thinks that a conversation between two housewives about the bargains to be found in the local store makes a good radio commercial simply isn't trying.

Outdoor advertising

The main feature of the outdoor advertising message has already been mentioned: except in certain specialized locations, it must be capable of being registered instantaneously. In practice, this means that there is no room for more than a headline and a visual; but, paradoxically, this limitation has produced the most dramatic and successful creative effects. This is a field where wit, both verbal and visual, is at a premium; fortunately, however, it is one where both are often found because poster advertising, with its potential for large-scale impact, has an irresistible appeal to many agency art directors.

9 Into production

Making a TV commercial

Television advertising is expensive, not only because of the cost of buying time, but also because the making of the commercials themselves is costly. A 30-second commercial can cost over £30 000 to produce, which is equivalent to a budget of over £7 million for a full-length feature film; and the use of exotic locations or well-known performers pushes the cost even higher. This is a problem that some advertisers have never satisfactorily solved. Having spent a great deal on production, the natural instinct is to justify the production expense by giving the commercial plenty of exposure – but then the advertiser comes up against the cost of time. At the same time, production of commercials grows more and more sophisticated as advertisers vie with one another to fight for the viewer's attention. This competitiveness tends to freeze out the middle range of advertisers, forcing them either to make cheaper commercials or to buy the less expensive slots or time packages. From time to time, there are murmurs in the advertising business that production companies and programme companies between them are killing off some of the lesser geese; but the fact is that no advertiser in the mass market can do without television advertising and many in other sectors would feel diminished if they did so. By way of compromise, in recent years there has been a distinct trend towards the use of simple settings rather than, say, action set on a beach in Bermuda, and replacement of actors by puppets, cartoon characters or other artefacts. While animation costs are high, they are paid for once-and-for-all, unlike actors who receive repeat fees.

An agency creative team setting out to produce a TV commercial

will have very little to go on. The writer and art director will have
some idea of what the production budget is likely to be – though not,
at this stage, in any detail. Often, in fact, the creative team produces
what amounts to an ideal script which is then 'budgeted down' to
the target figure.

The script

The basic document from which production begins is the script.
This may result from days of batting ideas to and fro in the creative
team's office or, more rarely, from a Eureka-style piece of inspiration
in the bath. (The copywriter for the 'Heineken refreshes the
parts . . .' ads is said to have awoken in the middle of the night with
the idea.) But the idea is only the beginning. What are you going to
do with it? How is it to be treated, illustrated, accompanied? From
these questions a series of further ideas will gradually emerge from
the mist and be expressed in a succession of draft scripts, many of
which will be discarded while others are polished and improved.
Eventually a definitive draft script will be produced, given a working
title (which will be for internal use only) and showing the visuals
alongside the accompanying dialogue, voiceover, music, sound
effects and so on. At this stage, the creative team may feel sufficiently
satisfied – though what they have produced so far may well be only
a shadow of the final version – to show their work to their creative
head and probably to other directors of the agency.

Storyboards and animatics

The next stage is to present the script to the client. A script is a
semi-technical document which is not easily 'readable' outside the
business, so agencies usually provide themselves with 'props' to
help in their presentations.

The basic and oldest-established prop is the storyboard – a
sequence of roughly drawn pictures which show the development
of the storyline, highlighting significant points in the action. A more
sophisticated version is the 'animatic', which can give an impression
very close indeed to the finished commercial. The storyboard pictures are drawn in fairly close detail, photographed individually to

make up a sequence of stills, and sometimes presented with a sound track. An animatic serves a double purpose, since it can be used not only to demonstrate the proposed commercial to the client but also as a sample to try out on groups of consumers. A technically more finished form of the animatic is sometimes used for actual commercials, drawing-board and laboratory time being notably less expensive than outside location camera crews and actors.

The production of 'dummy' commercials for evaluation and testing probably stands to gain over the next few years by the spread of computer graphics of the kind regularly seen in news and current affairs television programmes, in which varieties of images can be simply created by a couple of people working at a console. It would be surprising if this form of language did not join the languages of film in all their variants to add another medium to the palette of the producer of TV commercials.

Clearance

In Britain, television advertising is strictly controlled by a number of statutory and voluntary regulations and codes of practice. (Controls on advertising in general are discussed at length in the next chapter.) These govern not only what may and may not be advertised on television (cigarette and charity advertising being probably the best-known prohibitions) but also *how* certain products may be presented, and what kinds of claims may be made for them. Clearly, it makes sense to have the scripts of commercials vetted before production costs are incurred, and this clearance process is carried out by the Independent Television Companies Association, representing the sixteen independent contractors who are, in the end, responsible to the Independent Broadcasting Authority for observing the IBA's requirements as well as the Broadcasting Act. In fact, the clearance certificate that each commercial has to earn before it can be publicly shown is awarded only after the ITCA has viewed the finished product; but most commercials are presented initially to the ITCA in script form and discussed, often in great detail, with the agencies at that stage. The ITCA may well give general approval to a script while drawing attention to points – for example, in connection with the use of child or teenage characters – which should be watched in the course of production; and in this case these points will be scrutinized closely when the finished commercial comes up for viewing. Rejection at this stage is by no means unknown, and the ITCA is regarded with wary respect by people in advertising.

Production

At this point in the production of a commercial, the big money begins to flow. The ideal lead time, from getting estimates to transmission, is between twelve and sixteen weeks, but in fact most commercials are produced in a much shorter period (and, as a result, their costs rise, since shorter schedules tend to involve film crew overtime, 24-hour processing work, and other expensive contingencies).

As explained in Chapter 7, even those advertising agencies which have so-called TV Production Departments do not, in fact, produce commercials themselves. They take charge of the production, but the work itself is done by production companies, many of which specialize in particular types of commercials. Estimates for production are usually obtained from two or three such companies, though it is likely that the agency's creative team will have a good idea of which they would like to do the job. For all that it often has to be done in a hurry, estimating for a commercial is a fiendishly complex task, involving as it does so many different elements, from performers to set carpenters, and, in the case of outdoor locations, so many imponderables like the weather, aircraft or traffic noise, or vehicle breakdowns. Anyone who has ever done any film or TV work will know how large a number of people is required (partly to satisfy union rules) for a relatively simple scene – typically, up to about twenty. Then there is the cost of studio and lab work: sound mixing, dubbing, processing, adding artwork titles or even special effects. All these involve using highly paid professionals working in high-rent premises. Music may have to be specially commissioned, or copyright fees on existing music be allowed for. Each showing of a commercial attracts a repeat fee for an actor appearing in it. And so the total production cost builds up.

By about four weeks into the production schedule, the cast will have been chosen, the sets built or the outdoor locations found, and all will be ready for shooting. For a 30-second commercial, this may take two days or as many as five. Shooting will be attended by the agency creative team involved, who may have to make last-minute changes or adjudicate on extra costs if problems come up, and, if the agency is out of luck, by the client. The result of the shooting will be much more film than it is intended to use: there will be takes where someone fluffs his lines or gets in the way of the camera; several different takes of the same scene of which one is to be chosen; takes deliberately allowed to run so that the best bit can be edited later. A typical shoot for a 60-second commercial will produce an hour or so of film, known as the 'rushes'.

The rushes contain the material on sound and vision, kept separate at this stage so that any part can be matched with any other, from which the 'rough cut' is made. This is the first, roughly edited version of the finished commercial, though lacking at this stage such optical effects as dissolves, fades and wipes, artwork and other special effects. To the average viewer of finished commercials, buffed up and with all the rough edges taken off, the 'rough cut' would look very rough indeed.

Post-production

At this point, before the final production and processing work, the client is usually called in to give his approval. Then comes the final cleaning-up and tidying operation: grading the film by means of filters so that the colour quality is consistent throughout, adding artwork and effects, marrying up and correcting the sound input, and ending up with a 'married print'.

Two or even more versions of the commercial may emerge from all this. One of the devices increasingly used to ease the cost of television time is to show the full version of a commercial a couple of times, say, during the day, and then to reinforce the message with shorter ten-second versions containing the punch-line. If this is the plan, the shorter version has, of course, to be edited and put together separately, and distributed to the TV companies as a separate item.

For many years, the final format of many commercials has been on videotape, the transfer from film being made at the end of the post-production process; though many advertisers and agencies still insist that the quality of the film image, even when seen on a television screen, makes the cost of producing prints (far higher than for videotape copies) worthwhile for each TV station. Increasingly, however, videotape is being used earlier in production; as videotape standards improve, this trend can be expected to grow. One of the plus factors is the ease (and therefore the relatively low cost) of adding opticals. It may well be that making commercials on film will soon be a thing of the past, though this depends on the development of high-quality portable video equipment for location work. Already the use of videotape for certain kinds of commercials, such as those for newspapers which depend on quick production and the inclusion of topical material, is routine.

The final stages

Once the commercial has received its clearance certificate from ITCA, it is ready for distribution. The mechanics of getting the commercial to the TV stations varies. The oldest-established method, dating from the 1950s when videotape was in its foggy infancy, is to supply 'bulk prints' on film. Since each station requires six prints, this involves a total of almost 100 copies and is an added expense. A cheaper and now more common method is to supply each station with a master tape from which it makes its own copies. For such 'instant' commercials as those trailing the contents of the next day's newspapers, there are facilities for sending them 'down the line' through the transmission network. Normally, however, commercials are expected to be with the station a week in advance of transmission.

There is one final check at the TV stations before commercials go out. The stations' traffic departments are responsible for making up the batches of commercials, and as transmission time draws near they keep a close eye on possible embarrassments; for example, an item in the news such as political trouble abroad or an air crash might make certain commercials inappropriate and in bad taste, and in that case they would not be broadcast.

TV advertising on the cheap

Not all TV commercials, of course, cost upwards of £30 000 to produce or are made in the sophisticated, quality-controlled way described above. It is not only that many advertisers cannot afford that kind of expense; some messages simply do not justify it. A department store holding its January sale needs to get across only the basic fact of when the sale starts; its name and reputation will be well enough known in its shopping catchment area. All that is needed in this case is an artwork slide announcing Bloggs' Winter Sale and a voiceover giving the starting date. Basic ads of this sort are the bread and butter of regional TV stations. Used as 'fillers' and sold on a run-of-programme basis, they are an effective and cheap medium, especially for retail trades.

Between this very basic kind of commercial and the full-blown 30-second or longer 'storyline' ad there is an infinite number of variations; examples of many of them can be seen in a single evening's ITV viewing.

Creating press ads

Press ads range from a simple announcement about a product to the detailed specification of a new car. They may be informative, or they may be designed to express a mood (as in 'fragrance' advertising) or a style (as in ads for designer jeans). Naturally, the process of creating press ads depends on the kind of message, the medium to be used, the amount of production work involved – artwork, photography and so on – and the amount of money the advertiser is prepared to spend.

Within any budget, there are always a number of options. The advertiser may want to make a big splash, concentrating the campaign over a short period to coincide with, say, the August car-buying boom or the spring rush of home decorating, or he may choose a series of 'bursts' over a longer period. The advertising may have to coincide with other aspects of the total marketing strategy, such as in-store merchandising or a public relations effort. Only when the media detail and the timing have been worked out can the creative team get down to business.

As with TV commercials, the basic theme of press advertising may be the result of inspiration or sweat, according to the creative people's style and luck. Sometimes the advertiser may know what he wants to say; in other instances it may be for the creative team to make suggestions. It is common for copywriters and art directors to visit factories and offices, watching the advertiser's operation closely in search of an angle. When advertisements state, say, that twenty-four different inspectors check a product before it is pronounced fit to sell, or that certified health inspectors check the propriety of every pea before it is frozen, this is an indication that some such works visit has taken place.

Eventually, the idea for a press ad – or for a series – emerges in the form of a 'scamp' – a scribbled rough sketched out on a sheet of paper showing, perhaps, a headline and an outline of the artwork or photograph. Tossed around in the agency between copywriter, art director, creative head and the account team, this will gradually be refined to the point where it can be 'worked up' to a more finished state for presentation to the client. This working-up stage is the responsibility of a 'visualizer', a rather confusing description since his job is to turn a 'scamp' into a 'visual', not to do any original visualization. According to the practice of the agency and the expectations of the client, the visualizer may produce either a rough drawn in magic marker or a full-scale pen-and-ink job. The headline may be inked in roughly, or done more accurately with transfer lettering. A number of different versions may be produced, not only to show alternative treatments but also to show how spaces of different sizes and proportions will be used.

Meanwhile the copywriter will have been working on the body copy, which will have gone through a similar process of refinement. When everything is ready – probably with the clock apparently ticking faster as deadline time approaches – the agency unveils its proposals to the client.

Conflicts and problems

In practice, quite apart from the perennial problem in the advertising business of shortage of time, the creative process is rarely as simple as that. Some agencies thrive on the tensions between their various departments, adopting the fashionable style of aggressive management. But even if they do not, there are inevitable conflicts, notably between design and copy. Many writers instinctively believe that art directors want to over-design and tend to submerge the message in technique. For their part, art directors accuse copywriters of wanting to say too much and not allowing the art to do its fair share of the work. What are seen as frustrating constraints are sometimes imposed by the company policy of the client, for example in the use (and perhaps size) of the company logo. One large public company has a 48-page manual entirely devoted to the company logo and how it is to be used, together with precise colour specifications when it is used in colour.

Designers also have to work within the practicalities of production, bearing in mind that certain design effects are appropriate to different printing processes. It has to be said here that, just occasionally, moments of madness slip through, such as red overprinting on a photograph, which becomes almost always unreadable. Many such difficulties can be learned only by experience, but most designers have a collection of 'don'ts' built up partly from bitter memories, phobias and prejudice. Here is a typical selection culled from the conversation of one designer, though probably no other would agree with all of them:

* In web-offset printing, green is notoriously inconsistent and tends to 'fall away' during the print run.
* Avoid reversing out white-on-black in letterpress; the black is rarely a true black and the white lettering tends to 'fill in' and look smudgy.
* You never know in what position on the page an ad will appear, or whether it will be on a left-hand or right-hand page. Put the focal point of an illustration in the centre if possible, to cope with any eventuality.
* Avoid punctuation in a headline. It disturbs the balance of the typography.

> * A reader should never look at an ad and have to ask, 'What's this about?' It should tell him without asking.

In a well-managed agency, there will be controls to prevent the grosser errors creeping through. It is surprising, though, when one considers how many eyes are looking at ads during the creative and production stages, how many errors appear. The misuse of the apostrophe in the possessive 'its' is now fairly commonplace, even in headlines. As for design error, the prize must surely go to an ad which appeared in a national magazine with a 32 000 circulation during the month this chapter was being written. It is a beautifully laid-out and illustrated mail order ad for reproduction furniture. The copy is enticing and informative. The items are photographed in good colour, displayed in panels alongside copy reversed out white on black. The only trouble is that the reply coupon, too, is reversed out, so that one would need a white felt-tip pen to complete it.

Satisfying the client

Interpreting the hopes and needs of the client, and bringing these together with the efforts of the creative team, is one of the functions of agency account management. There are, however, psychological factors that can get in the way of a harmonious relationship, and these often come out when an agency puts up its ideas at a presentation. The client's image of his own company may be made up of many complex and sometimes conflicting elements: loyalty, company history, trade reputation, the 'new broom' ambitions of a young management team, and so on. An old-established chocolate manufacturer, for example, will believe (and he may be right, up to a point) that no one knows chocolate or consumers of chocolate as well as he does. The agency team are outsiders, unadmitted to the charmed chocolate circle. They may have researched the market, toured the factory, studied the sales figures and interviewed everyone from the managing director to the chargehand on the chocolate cream line, but chocolate is not their life, as it is the client's.

For their part, the creative team may well feel that the client is lacking a spirit of adventure, hidebound by old conventions, or just plain misguided. Highly original ideas sometimes get shot down because the client prefers to do something similar to his competitors. There is a terrible contagion, amounting almost to a disease of the imagination, in some industries, says an agency creative head, citing brewing as an example. 'The average drinker,' he goes on, 'thinks lagers all taste pretty much the same. That's a good reason for making sure that at least lager ads don't all look the same. But what do you get?' It's fair to add that his agency doesn't have a lager account.

A client difficulty that particularly afflicts agencies with smaller clients is that it is not easy, without considerable experience, to translate the rough of an ad into an image of what the finished ad will look like. One way round this, of course, it to present something closer to the finished version, and this is standard practice in some large agencies with big-spending clients. The small agency, however, is in a dilemma. Finished work costs money which may well turn out to be a dead loss. But if there is too much of a gap between what the client perceives and what he gets, he may move to another agency. This is where the agency/client relationship is vital, and it is one reason why some agencies prefer to remain small, remaining in a world of a size where they feel in control, rather than venturing into the more uncertain big time.

How much will it cost?

Once the client's approval has been obtained, the next stage is to produce a detailed estimate according to the budget. At the very simplest, this will consist of the cost of typesetting and of space in the media chosen. However, for, say, an ad for suntan lotion involving location photography it will be far more complex. The photographer, one or more models, a dresser, hairdresser and make-up artist will have to be hired, transport and accommodation arranged, and film and processing paid for. It may be necessary to have a lighting man on hand. Then there is the cost of studio work: making up the transparencies with the other elements of the ad, retouching the transparencies to remove blemishes, re-processing to improve the colour balance, and separation of the finished artwork into four colours. All this will add up to several thousand pounds, before a single inch of space has been booked.

The estimate has, of course, to receive client approval before production can go ahead.

Production for the press

Items supplied to a newspaper or magazine for reproduction as an advertisement are called 'mechanicals'. At the most sophisticated level – say for a full-colour ad for suntan lotion in a glossy magazine – the mechanical will be a complete piece of artwork, separated by overlays into four colours: blue (known to printers as cyan), yellow, red (magenta) and black. At the other extreme there may be some copy for setting 'in house', plus perhaps a copy of a company logo.

At the level of local newspapers and small-circulation magazines, much advertising is 'pub. set' – that is, the headline and copy is sent to the paper, and the typesetting and layout are done there. With luck, the agency or client may see a proof before printing goes ahead. But this practice is dying out even at the lower reaches of advertising, because most people have realized that since pub. setting and layout are charged extra, it is possible to get better results and achieve greater control by using the independent typesetters and layout studios which are now available in towns of any size, at little extra cost, if any. No advertiser of any stature would allow himself to submit to the vagaries of pub. set work, with the exception of a small panel giving details of a local dealer, a common feature of car and hi-fi ads. The new printing technology has encouraged the use of direct artwork. In the old days it was necessary to go to the expense of producing a block which was then sent on to the newspaper or magazine. Now that most papers (even in Fleet Street) and magazines are made up in the form of page-by-page artwork which is then converted into printing plates, advertising artwork submitted can be pasted direct on to the page without additional cost.

No advertising agency, even the largest, has in-the-house facilities for producing the wide range of different types of mechanicals that it handles. While physical production of an ad will be closely supervised and checked by the art director or, in a larger agency, by the production department, it will be done outside – sometimes, in a number of different houses, typography going to one place, layout to another, and so on. In agencies large enough to have a traffic department, responsibility rests there for bringing together all these separate operations, as well as for getting approval of the proofs at each stage from inside the agency and from the client.

It must be remembered that few advertising campaigns involve one advertisement appearing on one occasion in one publication. Depending on the campaign strategy, there may be a series of ads to appear in their ordained order in a variety of publications, each of which will have their own deadlines for delivery of artwork, proofing, clearance of proofs, and so on; and each of which may be reproduced in different dimensions. The organization of all this demands the same kind of skills as the composition of a railway timetable, and it is one of the less obvious services provided by the advertising agency.

Handling proofs

It is necessary here to put in a word for the uninitiated who have not had the experience of handling proofs. These are not, as is often assumed, the printer's first efforts, with which agency or client may tamper at will. Any doubts about the copy, the position of the head-line, the placing of the logo or any other matter within the control of the originator of the ad should have been resolved at or before finished artwork stage. Proofs are in the nature of a confirmation that the instructions to the printer have been carried out. As proofs are customarily supplied on paper far superior to what will be used in the actual printing, it is hazardous even to comment on the quality of colour or the depth of ink. It does happen that, in a full-colour ad, one or other of the colour plates needs to be 'taken back' a shade or so but, in general, provided the original artwork was right, so will the proof be. Small-business clients often need to be restrained at the proof stage, being often tempted to second thoughts. While it is possible, and I have seen it done, to halt the printing of a magazine once it is on the machine in order to expunge an intrusive piece of punctuation, this is unlikely to endear the perpetrator to the printers, and the cost of the stoppage will appear in the final print bill.

Buying print

In press advertising, the actual printing is taken care of by the medium used, and the cost is part of the price of space. There are, however, other forms of advertising in which the agency – or the advertiser, if he is working direct – has to buy the print itself. Posters are one example; others are mail order catalogues, direct mail shots, brochures, and other pieces of promotional material that may need to be produced.

These days, the cardinal rule in dealing with printers is to keep everything except the actual running-off of copies out of their hands. This may seem unkind, but it is a fact of life that the price of the technological revolution that has overtaken printing in the past twenty years has been the printers' total reliance on, and faith in, the machine. The day of the erudite printer's reader who would ring you up to query the placing of a comma or the spelling of the name of an obscure oasis in the Sahara is past. If typesetting is read at all at the printer's, it will be read against the original copy, which will be faithfully reproduced. Fortunately, this loss has been compensated for by the thousands of little typesetting outfits that have sprung up, largely dependent on short order work and their own efficiency. While you can hand over all the copy and illustrations for, say, a mail order catalogue to a printer and let him make of it what he will, you will obtain a better product by separating the design, typesetting and make-up functions, and farming them out. All the printer has to do then is to make the plates and run off the copies.

The thirst for printed product has spawned two distinct types of new business in recent years: one is the instant print shop; the other is the format printer, who will produce brochures and other material in one of a range of stylized formats at what looks like a bargain price. The instant print shop has its uses, though their in-house typesetters and designers are not always the best available, even in a small provincial town; and, if left to themselves, they tend to produce material which is in their own house style rather than the client's. Format printers offer little scope for the establishment of a company style; by shopping around, their prices can usually be matched by printers who allow you to devise your own style of presentation.

Although it is customary to invite two or three quotations for any print job of any size, most people in the advertising business remain faithful to a small number of suppliers of typesetting, finished art-work and machining. One good reason for this is that it is easier to ask someone to stay late to meet a deadline if you have put business that way before and can be expected to do so again. Clients should not be allowed to suggest their own favourite printers; that way, you are never quite sure who is the printer and who the supplier.

None of this applies to the printing of posters for large sites. There is only a handful of printers doing this kind of work anyway, and it is to a large extent a seller's market. Nevertheless, the responsibility for colour quality and sheet-to-sheet matching, and for the checking of proofs, rests with the agency. The distribution of posters and subsequent checking of their condition is in the hands of the poster contractors.

Radio production

In radio, as elsewhere, the style of commercials varies widely. A national commercial, distributed to ILR stations, may well use the voice of a famous personality and be similar in quality to the sound-track of a TV advertisement. At the other end of the scale, a local retailer's ad may consist of a few words recorded by one of the local station's presenters.

The difficulties of producing an effective radio commercial are often underestimated in Britain, with results that are only too pain-fully evident. The radio commercial has nothing to sustain it but how it *sounds*; there can be no atmospheric photography, no manipulation of puppets, no optical special effects to hold it up. There it is: a snippet of noise, competing – as likely as not – with the washing machine, the Hoover, the prattle of children or the ambient sound of a traffic jam. Radio is more easily dismissed than television; you have only to switch off one sense to avoid it altogether. In terms of how much information can be got across, in what depth, radio's nearest equivalent is probably the poster.

An additional complication is that radio commercials are not so sharply differentiated from the programmes that surround them as those on television. The way round this recommended by many producers is to open with something that creates its own divide, a device known in the business as a 'bumper'. It may be a snatch of contrasting music, or an unusual sound effect, or even an unusual voice.

Radio production begins with an idea – let's say, the unique feature or USP of a particular brand of toothbrush – which is then developed into a script. Dialogue format is common, perhaps too common, in radio commercials, and one way of bringing out the toothbrush's USP would be to have two mothers discussing their choice of toothbrushes for their children. But this is pretty hackneyed; how many housewives have we heard in ads comparing floor cleaners, instant coffee brands, face lotions, and practically everything else? So the discussion in the agency might go: why not have two *children* talking about their toothbrushes? This would allow for some humour and warmth in the script.

Scripts can either be written inside an agency or farmed out to the company that will eventually produce the tape. Either way, the client's approval is sought at the finished script stage, though in the case of a series an agency might venture the expense of a sample tape. The big expense in radio production, in relation to the total cost, is studio time, and efforts are usually made by way of thorough preparation to keep this as short as possible. The finished commercials are distributed to the radio stations on cassette or cartridge, or occasionally, in the case of topical material, direct over the IBA network.

For purely local radio commercials, the station's own studio facilities may be used, though these are generally suitable for only the most basic announcements of the 'Hurry on down to Bloggs' sale' type. Towns and cities of a size large enough to carry an ILR station usually have independent producers who can cope with more complicated requirements.

Radio commercials are subject to controls, though these are less strict than those for television. They are described in the chapter which follows our final visit to our would-be advertisers.

Case histories: 3

It is time to see how our three sample advertisers are getting on. We left them, you will remember, about to embark on their advertising campaigns, armed as they were with basic research on their problems and aims.

Chase

Chase's agency, ABCD, proposed a campaign aimed at 15–24-year-olds buying Chase for themselves, and young mothers buying Chase as a snack for their children. The emphasis was to be on Chase's 'sustaining' and 'quick energy' qualities, with some reference to its being 'easy to eat'.

At once, ABCD has a problem. The young mothers are bang in the target area for a TV campaign, but 15–24-year-olds are light viewers and unlikely to be reached in large numbers in this way. It was decided to suggest outdoor advertising – posters and bus sides – for the younger target audience.

First, ABCD tackled the problem of ridding Chase of its 1930s image. One suggestion was to rename the product Chaser, which lent itself to a number of storyline possibilities; but this was vetoed by the client. 'Chaser' was a word associated with alcohol, and therefore inappropriate for a product aimed at a young market. Brooding on all this, the creative team realized that what the word 'Chase' signified was *movement*. The result was a number of versions of the word: in italics, with a streak of light running through it, with the letters on wheels, and so on. Then, one day, the art director wrote the word on his pad and idly put an ellipse (three dots) after it: 'Chase . . .' Still doodling, he enlarged the dots until they were spots slightly smaller than the lettering.

'What are the three blobs for?' asked the copywriter.

'Oh, I don't know. What about "sustenance", "quick energy" and . . .'

'. . . Easy to eat?'

That was the starting-point of the Chase campaign. A couple of days later, the creative team had come up with the following ideas for television:

> *Scene: A mother is packing her ten-year-old's lunch-box. She puts in sandwiches, an apple, a plastic bottle of drink. Then she holds out a Chase.*
>
> MOTHER: And Chase?
>
> CHILD: What are the three spots for?
>
> MOTHER [*smiles; they both know the game*]: Nourishment. Energy. And . . .
>
> CHILD and MOTHER [*together*]: Something extra!
>
> *Scene: Children in playground, inspecting their lunch-boxes.*
>
> FIRST CHILD: What have you got?
>
> SECOND CHILD [*turning over contents of lunch-box*]: Sandwiches again! Oh, a banana. Goody. And look, Chase.
>
> FIRST CHILD: Chase? What are the three spots for?
>
> SECOND CHILD [*witheringly*]: Nourishment. Energy. And, um . . .
>
> FIRST CHILD: Something extra?
>
> *Scene: Teenage boy and girl out cycling. They have stopped by a signpost ('Sleepy Hollow, 2').*
>
> BOY: Oh, no! Another two miles!
>
> GIRL: Never mind, let's have a rest. Look! [*She holds up a Chase.*]
>
> BOY: Chase. What are the three spots for?
>
> GIRL: Nourishment. Energy. And . . .
>
> BOY: Yeah?
>
> GIRL [*breaking off a piece for him*]: Something extra. [*She smiles at him.*]
>
> BOY [*looking steadily at her*]: Something extra. Yeah.

For the posters ABCD proposed a two-part campaign. First, a

packshot of Chase, with a large headline: 'WHAT ARE THE THREE SPOTS FOR?' A month later, the answer: 'Nourishment. Energy. And something extra.'

The TV ideas were fairly simple, so for the client presentation ABCD prepared a storyboard for each, with captions underneath showing the dialogue, together with complete draft scripts. An in-house artist drew mock-ups of the posters, showing them 'straight' and also in a number of street scenes. There were elongated versions for the bus sides.

The client's initial response was sticky. The marketing manager wanted the 'easy to eat' angle emphasized. No one liked the third TV idea, which might be thought suggestive, and in any case might not get ITCA clearance. But the most important objection was to the 'three spots'. In the 15–24 part of the target audience, someone pointed out, 'spots' meant acne; the ad might be taken to mean that Chase gives you spots. In any case, you know what kids are like; they'd make a joke of it, anyway.

'Dots?' suggested the copywriter.

'Not much difference. And they're not dots. They're bigger than dots.'

'Arrows?'

'Why?'

The copywriter had been harking back to his idea about movement, but he didn't pursue it.

'What about stars?' said the art director. ' "What are the three stars for?" '

The meeting ended with agreement on 'three stars' and instructions to ABCD to come up with another idea for the teenage ad. The marketing man's worries about the 'easy to eat' angle vanished when someone from ABCD pointed out that any chocolate bar was easy to eat, and it was therefore a waste of time and money saying so.

The creative team's revised ideas for the teenage ad were:

> Scene *as before, but with two girls (16 or so).*
> FIRST GIRL: Oh, no! Another two miles!
> SECOND GIRL: Never mind, let's have a rest. Look! [*She holds up a Chase.*]
> FIRST GIRL: Chase. What are the three stars for?
> SECOND GIRL: Nourishment. Energy. And . . .

FIRST GIRL: Something extra?

SECOND GIRL: That's right.

[*Second girl breaks the Chase in half and hands half to first girl. Camera moves to show a steep hill ahead.*]

VOICEOVER: When you need something extra. Chase. [*Packshot.*]

Scene: 'Top of the Form' type TV quiz show.

QUESTION-MASTER: Now, in this round, I'll take answers from any member of the team.

[*Camera shows three tense team-members.*]

QUESTION-MASTER: For three points. I have here a well-known chocolate bar. And the question is, what are the three stars for?

[*All buzzers sound together.*]

[*Camera pans to each team member in turn.*]

FIRST BOY: Nourishment.

GIRL: Energy.

SECOND BOY [*hesitantly*]: Something extra?

[*Indicator shows three points. Applause.*]

VOICEOVER: Three-star value. Chase.

[*Packshot.*]

The ABCD team were still keen on the 'Sleepy Hollow' idea, and the alternative was put forward only as a target. There would be predictable difficulties over transmission, since the IBA would not allow any possibility of confusion between the commercial and any programme it might be shown within, or adjacent to. As expected, the client accepted the revised version of 'Sleepy Hollow'.

Before developing the drafts into full pre-production scripts, it was decided to test consumer reaction with groups of 15–24-year-olds and young mothers. For cheapness and speed, the medium used was slides taken from the storyboard, plus a mocked-up sound track. The work was farmed out to a research company with whom ABCD had worked in the past. Here are some of the comments made:

15–24-year-olds

'Might try it. It looks different.'

'What about the calories?'

'That's right. You need energy if you're on a bike.'

Young mothers

'They need something to help them get through the day.'

'It's like a treat, isn't it – after the sandwiches.'

'Gives them something to look forward to.'

'Chocolate for energy – that's well known.'

The next stage was to write a full script and submit it for clearance. ITCA noted that it should be made clear that the drink in the 10-year-old's lunch-box was in a *plastic* bottle, in line with the IBA requirement that 'any situations in which children are to be seen or heard in advertisements should be carefully considered from the point of view of safety'. ABCD were also reminded, as a matter of routine, of the provisions of the Children (Performances) Regulations 1968 on the employment of child actors.

It had been agreed with the client that the campaign would be tested in two ITV regions, posters also being used in those areas. The commercials would be run for two months, covering both phases of the poster campaign. ABCD obtained estimates for producing the commercials from two companies, both of whom were known for their work with children; they then put the winning estimate together with the TV time, poster production and contract costs, to make a total estimate for the client. This was agreed with the client's budget.

Using simple sets, only two actors in each story and no expensive special effects, production of the commercials was relatively cheap and fast. By the time they were back at ITCA for clearance, the first version of the poster was being distributed throughout the test areas by the contractor. ABCD favoured taking every advantage of the photogenic appeal of the child actors, so the commercials were to be transmitted from film. Prints were made and distributed to the two regional ITV companies.

Meanwhile, back at the Chase factory, the marketing department had been working to ensure that the increased demand in the test areas would be satisfied. The point-of-sale material distributed to shops included a display rack with a header carrying the words: 'WHAT ARE THE THREE STARS FOR?' This was to ensure that Chase kept its own status as a nourishing snack and would not be confused in the customers' minds with 'sweets'. Marketing activity was supported by advertisements in the appropriate trade papers.

If Chase were a real product, the rest would be history. The test campaign, having proved successful, would have been extended to cover the whole country. Further commercials, all using the line 'What are the three stars for?', and further posters would have been produced. And the makers of Chase, having rescued their flagship product from the doldrums, would have rejoiced.

Taplow's Hardware

Robert Taplow's friend at Y and Z Publicity listened carefully to Robert's explanation of his problem. Robert was not overly ambitious; he merely wanted a share of the do-it-yourself market, in the areas covered by the three shops, that would make the shops viable.

Y and Z Publicity's first comment concerned the word 'Hardware'. It was wrong, he felt, both for today and for the kind of goods Robert most wanted to sell. He suggested that any advertising should be based simply on the word 'Taplow's', and that the shopfronts and business stationery should be brought into line, with a house style common to them all. This style would also be prominent in the ads.

Taplows' selling proposition was identified as 'service'. Graham Young, of Y and Z Publicity, asked Robert what kinds of advice customers asked for. Robert quoted a few examples, mentioning the kinds of 'tricks of the trade' that Taplow's staff passed on. Young, of necessity a home decorator himself, listened with interest.

'Could we put together a series of those?' he asked. 'You know, "Tips from Taplow's", something like that?'

Robert came back two days later with about a dozen ideas.

Graham Young explained that he had in mind a series of six ads. Each one would feature a 'Tip from Taplow's' in strip form. The spaces need not be large, and the cartoon format would make the ads stand out, even on the local paper's crowded pages.

'You might throw in a discount offer,' Graham suggested. 'Ten per cent off if you produce this ad – that kind of thing.'

'How much is all this going to cost?' asked Robert cautiously, thinking of his father.

'Leave it with me. I'll ring you tomorrow,' said Graham.

The cost, when he rang, came as a pleasant surprise. Graham had negotiated a small series discount for a regular space in the *Thrapsley Guardian*, 5 cm across the full width of a page. The only extras would be the fee for a local illustrator Graham knew, plus a small amount of typesetting. Even Robert's father was not too dismayed, though Robert had to use his powers of persuasion over the 10 per cent discount.

The little Taplow campaign was timed to start in the spring, when every householder's fancy turns to thoughts of redecorating. By that time the shopfronts had been changed and the new stationery had been printed. In fact, few people claimed their 10 per cent discounts (and most of those, Robert's father noted with disgust, were old customers anyway) but there was a pleasing number of new faces in the shops. Robert was encouraged enough to extend 'Tips from Taplow's' through the summer, taking Graham Young's advice to use his ads to encourage people to take on jobs they possibly wouldn't have dared to tackle themselves. As a result, Taplow's have extended their range of stock – getting rid of some of the old, slow-selling lines to make room – and considerably increased the average value of each purchase at their shops. And all because, as the punchline of the ads in the *Thrapsley Guardian* puts it, 'Taplow's tell you how'.

Beaver Generators

Beaver had been presented with three possible ways of reaching the market for their new emergency generator: (i) direct mail; (ii) trade press advertising; and (iii) the trade exhibition.

Beaver's consultants took as the starting-point of their advertising strategy that Beaver was a new name in this highly specialized field. It must therefore first establish its credibility. The consultants proposed a series of 'teaser' ads in the trade press, gradually becoming more specific, and all inviting reader response. A direct-mail shot would be prepared for the respondents. As taking part in the trade exhibition was by far the most expensive of the options, it was suggested that this be held in reserve as a possibility for a later date.

The work of devising the ads was farmed out to a freelance creative team, who spent a day talking to Beaver's managing and sales directors. They also talked to a couple of computer professionals found by the consultants.

The proposal was for full-page ads in each monthly issue of two trade journals, for six months. The first would show a worried computer manager biting his nails because his power supply had broken down. The headline asked, 'Ever wished you had a standby?' At the bottom of the page was a coupon with a second headline above it: 'Ask Beaver'. The last in the series showed the new generator, with the headline, 'Your standby', and the coupon as before.

Beaver's directors liked the idea in general, but they made two points. First, they thought that a three-month series of ads would be sufficient to start with. (The page-rates for the trade journals had shaken them a little.) Secondly, they disliked and distrusted coupons. A few people, they argued, might tear the page out and hand it to their secretaries. A few might intend to later, and forget. Some of the secretaries would forget to send the coupon off. Why not ask the reader to phone for details, Beaver asked. They reckoned their sales office could cope with the extra calls.

So the coupon and its headline went out and, in its place, in good strong type, went the words, 'Talk to Beaver on . . .' followed by the phone number. Of the six ads that had been roughed out, another was chosen to make up the set of three. It showed a close-up of a computer console indicating power failure, with the headline: 'Never considered a standby?'

You will not be surprised to hear (for naturally these are all success stories) that Beaver had a gratifying response to the ads. This provided the company, as a bonus, with a mailing list of prospects all of whom, of course, received the first mailing shot, a follow-up mailing and, if there was still no response, a phone call for an appointment. By the time the next trade exhibition came round, Beaver were able to book a stand in the confident knowledge that they were no longer seen as 'new boys' in the computer business, and they were able to add some new names to an already very healthy order book.

10 Advertising under control

There can be few areas of commercial life that are subject to as much control as advertising. In Britain, the controls exist at four levels:

1. Over 50 Acts of Parliament contain restrictive clauses relevant to advertising. They range from the Broadcasting Act 1981, which controls all television and radio advertisements, to the Medicines Act 1968, which deals with advertising in its particular sector of business.
2. The advertising business operates its own voluntary controls through codes of conduct established by its constituent organizations.
3. Media owners – publishers, radio and television programme companies, poster contractors, and so on – have the right to refuse to take advertisements that they consider unsuitable. In addition, they operate a variety of schemes to check the bona fides and good trading practices of certain advertisers such as mail order companies.
4. Professional and trade organizations ranging from the Pharmaceutical Society of Great Britain to the Glass and Glazing Federation operate codes of conduct relevant to the activities of their members.

The result of all this is that advertisements should not appear that are offensive, deceptive, in bad taste, unsuitable for their particular audiences or readership, or simply illegal. Nevertheless, some advertisements in these categories do slip through this finely woven net. Illegal advertisements are relatively easy to deal with, and prosecutions under the Trade Descriptions Act 1968, or one of the other Acts which make the advertising of misleading information a criminal offence, are fairly common. It is less easy to deal absolutely with such concepts as 'offence' and 'bad taste', since these are subjective judgements; but experience and precedent provide guidance to the controlling organizations, and an appreciation has built up over the years of the areas where offence is likely to be given. At the same time, advertisements in these contentious areas are under continual review, since public attitudes are volatile.

Television

As might be expected, given the power of television, its huge audiences, and the widespread awe in which the medium is held by virtually every government in the world, television advertising has attracted the heaviest controls. In Britain, radio and television are the only media whose content, both editorial and advertising, is specifically governed by an Act of Parliament.

Under the Broadcasting Act 1981, the Independent Broadcasting Authority's duties include the drawing up of 'a Code governing standards and practice and prescribing the advertisements and methods of advertising to be prohibited or prohibited in particular circumstances' and the responsibility for seeing that the code is observed. The code applies not only to the content of advertisements but also to the way in which the programme companies broadcast them. It is the IBA that lays down the proportion of advertising permitted (currently, on television, an average of six minutes per broadcasting hour, measured over the day, and not more than seven minutes in any one hour; on radio, nine minutes per hour average); the way in which advertisements must be differentiated from programmes; limits on the use of certain visual devices; and a wide range of other operational requirements.

Advertisements for charities or religions, or on subjects of political, industrial or other public controversy, are not permitted under any circumstances. Controls on the advertising of medicines and treatments are particularly severe, and include the prohibition of advertisements for pregnancy testing services and cures for smoking, for example. The use of children in advertisements, whether directed at other children or at the general audience, is strictly controlled, as is financial advertising. The IBA may impose restrictions on the times that certain advertisements may be broadcast; for example, advertisements for children's medicines, or showing children taking medicine, may not be televised before 9 p.m. or broadcast on radio in time slots which the IBA lays down.

Quite apart from these general restrictions, every TV commercial except for short local advertisements broadcast by only one programme company must be approved before transmission by the IBA. This approval does not, however, preclude any individual programme company from refusing to show any commercial, and from time to time companies do exercise this right.

Vetting

Clearly, it would be uneconomic to expect advertisers to risk the production cost of a commercial in the hope that it would receive IBA approval, and so, from the start of independent television in Britain in 1955, a 'vetting' system has been operated by the trade association of the programme companies, the Independent Television Companies Association. As explained earlier, this involves the inspection of production scripts and the elimination of possible clearance problems at that stage.

In 1985, the Copy Clearance Secretariat of ITCA read over 17 000 scripts for television commercials. (Many of these were re-submissions of revised scripts, so comparison of this figure with the number of commercials given clearance in their final form is not possible.) About 80 per cent of the scripts were given clearance with, at most, minor and uncontentious amendments. For example, ITCA objected to the word 'sway' in a beer commercial; other unacceptable practices might include the description of a biscuit having a 'thick' chocolate coating when it was not noticeably thicker than those of competitors' products, or the quotation of VAT-exclusive prices in a commercial for a retail product. ITCA requires the substantiation of any product claims or market research findings used in a script.

ITCA and the advertisers or their agents find themselves unable to agree on about 2 per cent of the scripts submitted. These are then referred to the ITCA Copy Committee, composed of senior programme company sales directors. If agreement still cannot be reached, the advertiser or agency is free to approach the IBA direct;

but in practice the Copy Committee is the final court of appeal for all but the most obstinate advertisers.

The script does not give a complete impression of a TV commercial. Much can happen during production that could make the final version unacceptable. An innocuous line in the script may, when filmed, be spoken in such a way as to suggest 'immoderate drinking', an offence against the IBA's code. A child actor following the script exactly may nevertheless appear to be ill-mannered or badly behaved, another contravention of the code. (Commercials for drink and those involving children are, in fact, agreed by ITCA to be the two most difficult areas.) Final clearance of a television advertisement is given only after ITCA and the IBA have jointly viewed the ready-for-transmission film or videotape. Sometimes ITCA may ask to see a double-headed version (with sound and vision not finally married together) so that any changes may be made with the minimum of expense.

Every morning at 9.45, ITCA and IBA staff view the new commercials for the day over a closed-circuit television link. Only if it survives this check is the commercial pronounced fit to be shown. About 10000 commercials a year go through this final test, and about 98 per cent of them are accepted without amendment. Many of the others need only slight changes.

The ITCA vetting system is entirely voluntary, operating in the interests of the honest advertiser and of the programme companies who of course have a concern that their audiences should be able to believe what they see and hear. It is financed by the programme companies. Although the Copy Committee exists as an appeal court, most of the work of clearance is done informally in discussion or by telephone, a swift turnround of scripts and resolution of any subsequent negotiations being essential in a business where deadlines are tight.

Radio

The Broadcasting Act also covers the programme and advertising content of independent local radio, for which the IBA is given responsibility. Although the IBA Code applies in broad terms equally to radio and television, restrictions on radio commercials are, in practice, rather more relaxed. This is partly because radio carries a higher proportion of local advertising (for which the stations themselves are responsible) and this tends to consist of unexceptionable retail announcements. Additionally, in a radio commercial there is less opportunity for unacceptable material to be introduced between the script and production stages. No doubt the more relaxed atmosphere surrounding radio advertising reflects the view of society in general that radio is less 'threatening' than television.

In radio, clearance for commercials is given at the script stage and there is no final production clearance, although local stations are required to check the finished commercial against its script. Commercials for use on only one station can be cleared by that station, the head of sales normally being the responsible 'clearer'. Where a commercial is to be carried by a small group of stations close together, as for example in the West Midlands where BRMB (Birmingham), Mercia Sound (Coventry) and Beacon Radio (Wolverhampton and the Black Country) share a small geographical area, they may nominate one of their heads of sales as the 'clearer' for all of them. Commercials which are to be broadcast nationally are subjected to a script clearance procedure similar to that for television.

The trade association of the local radio stations is the Association of Independent Radio Contractors (AIRC), which deputes its clearance duties to ITCA. ITCA's Copy Clearance Secretariat sees over 10000 radio scripts a year, though some of these are revised versions and some, for various reasons other than lack of clearance, do not actually reach transmission. The 'clearers' for individual or groups of stations may also refer to ITCA for an opinion on controversial or borderline scripts. AIRC says that the clearance system for radio commercials works well and 'is probably the least irksome and most helpful to companies of all the IBA regulatory areas'.

Complaints about broadcast advertising

The Independent Broadcasting Authority responds to, and indeed invites, complaints from the public about broadcast advertisements, each of which is investigated and replied to personally. Well over 1000 letters or telephone calls are received each year. Many of these, says the IBA, 'refer to matters of subsequent service or availability rather than copy context, and many – as might be expected – involve personal views rather than breaches of the Code. Matters of taste and decency, which are sometimes difficult to assess, and the inferences drawn from humour (even more difficult) are raised in a large proportion of letters.'

In a typical month, November 1985, the IBA received a total of 171 complaints referring to 110 advertisements. Of these, 45 were thought by the complainants to be misleading, 38 offensive and 17 harmful. 'Miscellaneous' accounted for the other 10. Personal disputes between customers and advertisers led to 18 complaints, some of which the IBA investigated with the advertisers. It is clear from the monthly summaries that the complaints procedure attracts considerable attention from minority activists. In November 1985, for example, two vegans complained about the promotion of milk by the Milk Marketing Board ('We cannot intervene on grounds of this kind,' said the IBA), while in July of the same year animal lovers protested about one commercial showing a snail with a punk haircut and another which showed a yoghurt pot falling from a fruit tree on to a hedgehog. (The IBA did not feel the need to intervene in these cases.) A number of complaints showed that viewers and listeners do not, in fact, view or listen carefully enough, believing themselves to have seen or heard things that were not there or alternatively failing to notice what was said. The prize for ingenuity must surely go to the student who, in November 1985, presented a complicated mathematical treatise concerning the amount of peppermint lost to the consumer because Polos have holes in them. ('There is no comparison on which to base anything misleading,' noted the IBA sympathetically.)

Apart from contacting advertisers over personal complaints, the IBA, in November 1985, agreed to watch closely the claims of service made by Datapost in any future campaign; to require a TV commercial offering a 'money-off' voucher, without stating that there was a minimum purchase condition, to be withdrawn; to require an apology over a misleading voucher offer by *TV Times*; to impose an after-7.30 p.m. restriction on a commercial described by a viewer as 'full of evil and violence', although the IBA noted that it was intended as satire; and to require half an hour's separation between a radio commercial featuring the singers Chas and Dave and a chat show in which they appeared. The advertisement attracting most complaints was one for a toy company which showed a child flying through the air holding the hand of a teddy bear. The 22 complainants feared that children would 'emulate what they saw and try flying out of bedroom windows'. The IBA contacted the advertiser, but pointed out that the commercial was not shown around programmes for small children, at the same time noting that the same objection might be made to Peter Pan.

The Advertising Standards Authority

The Advertising Standards Authority, set up in 1962, is a watchdog body which oversees all advertisements *except* those on radio or television. Complaints made to the ASA about broadcast advertising are passed on to the IBA.

The ASA is a voluntary body. Unlike the Independent Broadcasting Authority, it does not have the force of an Act of Parliament behind it; it also lacks the ultimate sanction, available to the IBA, of refusing to allow an advertisement to be used. In the end, nonbroadcast media owners make their own decisions; in practice, however, they (and advertisers and agencies) follow the ASA's advice. In many ways, the ASA is comparable with the Press Council, which deals with complaints about press editorial content. Both have an independent chairman and a majority of lay members. Both rely on the goodwill and co-operation of the media involved.

It would clearly be impracticable for the ASA to vet every press advertisement, every poster and every advertising film before it was used; the Authority's main functions are to see that the British Code of Advertising Practice is adhered to, and to deal with complaints from the public. (The Code is described later in this chapter.) The ASA does, however, check all advertisements for cigarettes before publication, and in practice most advertisements for alcoholic drinks are also pre-vetted. From time to time the Authority runs checks on advertisements for specific product ranges. It also operates a system of 'rolling' monitoring which brings all categories of press advertising under regular review.

Between 7000 and 8000 complaints are received each year from members of the public, a figure that has been fairly static for some years. If, after investigation, a complaint is upheld, the Authority seeks an assurance from the advertiser that the offence will not be repeated. Advertisers who do not respond to the ASA's inquiries or do not agree to amend their advertisements in line with the ASA's recommendations are reported to media owners.

The Authority issues a monthly *Case Report* which describes the complaints received and the action taken. As with the IBA, some complaints are in the nature of special pleading for minority interests or personal grievances against particular advertisers, or relate to general principles rather than to specific advertising content, or concern such problems as after-sales service. Some areas of contention in advertising, such as medical treatments, are excluded from radio and television by the IBA's Code, and it is therefore not surprising that these should figure prominently in the press and consequently in the complaints made to the ASA.

In a typical month (November 1985), the ASA received 586 complaints. Of these: 49 concerned broadcasting and were referred to the IBA; 84 were outside the ASA's remit because they were unrelated to advertising content; 115 involved no apparent breach of the British Code of Advertising Practice; 148 required further information from the complainants; and 88 of the complaints were already being, or had been, investigated. This left 102 complaints to be pursued.

The January 1986 *Case Report* gave the results of 109 investigations into breaches of the British Code of Advertising Practice which had been completed. The complaints were upheld in 70 instances, and partly upheld in a further three. Prominent among the complainants were readers who had been attracted by price offers in advertisements which turned out to involve hidden extra costs, or to have suffered increases since the advertisements were placed. Medical items included an advertisement for orthopaedic furniture which claimed to 'relieve naturally' a variety of conditions ranging from slipped disc to migraine (complaint upheld; claims not substantiated; media advised) and the claim of a practitioner of alternative medicine to heal cancer (complaint upheld; claims of cures for cancer not only breach the Code but are also an offence under the Cancer Act 1939; advertisement withdrawn). Holiday and hotel advertisements were also prominent.

Opinions of the protection afforded to consumers by the ASA vary widely. In 1978, a joint survey mounted by the Office of Fair Trading, the Consumers' Association and the ASA found only a small number of causes for complaint – and most of these were trivial – in a large sample of press advertising, and in 1980 a Department of Trade working party confirmed that the ASA system worked well. However, in 1983 the magazine *New Society*, a fairly consistent opponent of advertising (perhaps because it doesn't attract much apart from classified job ads), described the ASA's approach to offenders as 'pretty mealy-mouthed'. This was in a summary of a *Case Report* which picked out a handful of the jokier items. No doubt one's opinion as to whether an organization has teeth depends on whether one has been bitten; the view within advertising is that the ASA does indeed afford safeguards to the consumer and at times places restrictions on the advertiser. It must be admitted, though, that since most advertisements have appeared before any check is made, some damage to consumers' interests may have already been done before the advertiser is called to order. It is fair to add that, in a significant number of instances, advertisers who are approached by the ASA offer compensation to the complainants.

The ASA also oversees the operation of the British Code of Sales Promotion Practice (see below), which is concerned with premium offers, vouchers and similar sales inducements. In January 1986 *Case Report* reported on 25 claims of breaches against this Code, of which 15 were upheld. Subjects of complaint ranged from the refusal of stores to redeem vouchers obtained with earlier purchases (complaint upheld; complainant compensated) to the mailing of promotional literature relating to cigarettes to a 17-year-old girl (complaint not upheld; the girl had previously completed a coupon for an earlier promotion in which she had declared that she was over 18).

The British Code of Advertising Practice

Some 20 bodies with an interest in advertising are represented on the Code of Advertising Practice Committee, which was established in 1961 to provide a definitive guide to good practice. The British Code of Advertising Practice is updated from time to time, and the edition current at the time of writing, dated October 1985, is the seventh. The Code is, in effect, the rule-book for non-broadcast advertising, and it is the basis of the ASA's judgements on advertisement content.

The Code, which requires that it should be followed in the spirit as well as in the letter, lays down three principles of good advertising:

it should be legal, decent, honest and truthful;

it should show responsibility to the consumer and to society;

it should follow business principles of 'fair competition'.

In most areas of life in which compulsory or voluntary controls operate, they have been built up from experiences in the past. The BCAP is no exception. Its strictures on the advertising of medicines, for example, reflect the bad old days when advertisers could offer, as in a 1934 newspaper, 'Pills for all ailments. Never fail. Special 1s 3d.' There is now a long list of ailments on which no advertising is permitted, and a second list on which there are severe restrictions. Advertisements may claim to *relieve symptoms* of ailments, but not to cure them. The Code contains several pages of further restrictions on the advertising of medicines and health-related products. The long shadows of what E. S. Turner called 'the shocking history of advertising' can continually be seen stalking the 94 pages of the British Code of Advertising Practice.

Under the Code's general rules, the points covered include:

the use of models;

expressions of opinion;

political advertising;

the quotation of prices;

the use of the word 'free' and such phrases as 'prices from . . .';

testimonials and endorsements;

comparisons with other products.

Particular categories of products to which special rules apply include:

medicines, medical treatments, appliances, products and services related to health;

hair and scalp products;

vitamins and minerals;

slimming products and services;

cosmetics;

mail order and direct response advertising;

financial services and products;

advertisements offering employment or business opportunities;

advertisements addressed to children;

cigarettes;

alcoholic drinks.

The British Code of Sales Promotion Practice

This Code, established by the CAP Committee and supervised in operation by the ASA, is concerned with:

premium offers;

cut-price and free offers;

vouchers, coupons and samples;

promotions linked to charities;

promotions involving well-known personalities;

prizes and competitions.

Some examples of these kinds of promotions – those carried on product packs, for instance – do not involve advertisements; but many are publicized by advertising or form part of advertisements, and so a reference to this Code is necessary here. The Code also covers editorial promotional offers (for example, competitions run in association with particular companies) and applies also to some aspects of sponsorship.

Like the BCAP, the Code takes as its watchwords the requirement that sales promotions should be 'legal, decent, honest and truthful'. Applications for promotional products should be satisfied within 28 days, and damaged or faulty goods should be replaced, or any money refunded, without delay. A 'free' offer must indeed be free, subject only to postage or carriage charges. Other points from the Code include:

> Promotions with prizes. Three pages on the Code deal with the conditions of entry for such promotions, the announcement of results, the way in which such promotions are advertised, and the physical handling of entry forms, proofs of purchase, the judging and the distribution of prizes.

> Promotions to the trade or to employees.

It is clear from the complaints to the ASA about infringements of the British Code of Sales Promotion Practice that difficulties often arise because the staff of participating stores, including the staff of branches of chain stores, are not always aware of the promotions or of the conditions attached to them. There is clearly scope for better marketing of promotions within the trades concerned and for better in-store training, and it is perhaps surprising that the Code does not place more emphasis on this.

Direct marketing

The term 'direct marketing' includes direct mail (advertisements sent by post), direct response mail order advertising (where the reader sends for goods or information by post) and other direct response advertising. The trade body for this sector of business is the British Direct Marketing Association, which has its own Code of Practice.

The Code was introduced in January 1982 following one spectacular mail order collapse and a number of lesser ones which, combined with unfavourable coverage in radio and television consumer programmes, had shaken public confidence in shopping by post. Members of BDMA accept the British Code of Advertising Practice and the British Code of Sales Promotion Practice; the BDMA Code amplifies these in relation to the special conditions of direct marketing.

Again, the requirements of the Code reflect past history. Some of the earlier scandals of this sector of trade included advertisers who used accommodation addresses or temporary addresses from which they vanished as soon as a suitable amount of money had been received. The Code requires that if an accommodation address or Post Office box number is used for the consumer response, a company must also give in advertisements, catalogues and other sales material its actual postal address, at which it must provide staff to answer inquiries during office hours. A set of complex requirements on the advertising and supply of 'collectables' is an echo of the malpractices of the past when items were described as 'limited editions' when in fact they were not, and when hopes of an increase in value of items of supposed artistic value were raised recklessly.

The BDMA Code also covers telephone selling. Probably most people would welcome the outright banning of unsolicited telephone sales calls, but the BDMA permits them under certain rather vague conditions: for example, 'High pressure tactics shall be avoided.' As telephone selling is still a relative novelty in Britain, no doubt public pressure will, in time, force the BDMA to strengthen this section of the Code. Further sections deal with the fulfilment of orders (normally within 28 days), refunds (to be given without question if the goods are returned undamaged within seven days, or under the terms of any money-back guarantee that has been given), and the conduct of prize draws.

The BDMA operates a conciliation service for consumers who cannot reach a satisfactory solution in a dispute with the advertisers. This can lead, if necessary, to independent arbitration. However, the BDMA reports that its conciliation service deals with only about six cases a year, 'and these are usually due to misunderstandings which are very quickly cleared up'.

The Mailing Preference Service

Six trade organizations involved in direct mail operations run the Mailing Preference Service, which enables consumers to have their names removed from the mailing lists of participating companies, or alternatively, if they actually enjoy receiving unsolicited mail, to have their names added to the lists of mailers in a number of categories such as sport, travel, home and leisure. The Service was launched in 1983, and by 1985 there were over 100 participating companies, including such persistent mailers as the Automobile Association, Reader's Digest, the Consumers' Association and Time-Life. Up to March 1985, over 24000 people had asked for the removal of their names from lists, and 2500 had asked for their names to be added.

Mail order protection schemes

Mail order protection schemes are further controls on mail order advertisers, imposed in this case by media owners. They are operated by the Newspaper Publishers' Association (for the national papers), the Newspaper Society (for the provincial press) and the Periodical Publishers' Association (for magazines). There are slight variations in the different schemes, but they follow broadly the same pattern. They provide for the checking of mail order advertising copy, and advertisers are required to give a 'satisfaction or money back' guarantee. Advertisers are required to lodge a bond with the publishers from which unresolved claims can be met.

There are two important provisos to all these schemes. They apply only to sales made 'off the page', and not to purchases made from a catalogue sent for in response to an advertisement. Secondly, they apply only to display advertising, not to classified.

Publishers' controls

Media publishers are, of course, entitled to reject any advertisement if they think it likely to offend their readers, if they suspect the advertiser's bona fides, and indeed for any other, or for no, reason. One of the most celebrated examples in recent years was the refusal of some national newspapers to publish a Health Education Council ad for family planning clinics. It showed two interlocking pairs of feet, with a bubble near the female feet saying 'I hope he's careful' and one near the male feet saying 'I hope she's on the pill'. Ironically, the papers which refused to print the ad included those strongest on editorial prurience.

Statutory controls

Space does not permit a summary of all the Acts of Parliament and Statutory Instruments which have a bearing in the advertising business. The provisions of many of these are incorporated in the Codes of Practice mentioned earlier in this chapter, or in the Codes of Practice of the appropriate trade or professional organizations. For example, the Code of Practice of the Association of British Pharmaceutical Industries incorporates those sections of the Medicines Act 1968 which refer to the advertising of medicines both to the general public and to the medical and paramedical professions. Here, however, are brief notes on the major statutory controls:

* *The Trade Description Act 1968* treats advertising as an 'offer for sale' in the same sense as the display of goods in a shop and any label or ticket applied to them. It is an offence to give a false trade description to any goods offered for sale. For example, a sweatshirt described as 'pure cotton' must be made of 100 per cent cotton fibre with no man-made additives; a hotel claiming to have its

own golf course must indeed own it, not merely have an arrangement with a club next door.

* *The Consumer Transactions (Restrictions on Statements) Order 1976*, as amended, makes it an offence to word guarantees or conditions of sale in such a way as to diminish or remove the customer's rights at law, or in such a way as to lead the customer to believe that these rights are diminished or removed.

* *The Prices Act 1974* (and subsequent Orders) restricts the use of such terms as 'Bargain Offer', 'Sale Price' and so on to genuine reductions. Any 'usual price' quoted in an advertisement must be based on evidence that the item concerned has been on sale for a continuous period of 28 days within the previous six months.

* *The Food and Drugs Act 1955*, as amended, controls the use of certain terms in labelling and advertising food. For example, 'cream' must be real cream; and there are complex regulations covering the difference between fruit-flavoured drinks, fruit squashes, and fruit juices.

* *The Medicines Act 1968*, in addition to controlling the content of medicine advertisements both to the professions and to the public, includes controls on the depiction of medical or paramedical personnel, or suitably dressed models or actors, in such advertisements.

* *The Children (Performances) Regulations 1968* lays down strict conditions on the employment of children as models or actors. Those conditions are strengthened in some places by local authority by-laws.

* *The Consumer Credit Act 1974* (and subsequent regulations) requires all advertisements for credit, including loans and hire purchase, to give the cash and total credit prices of goods and the rate of interest that will be incurred by credit customers.

The controls imposed by consumer legislation such as the Trade

Description Act are carried out by local authority Trading Standards Officers (sometimes called Consumer Protection Officers), who may initiate prosecutions of advertisers and, if they choose, of their advertising agencies and of the media in which offences have been committed. However, since, in law, an agency's or a medium's 'reliance on information supplied' is an allowable defence, prosecutions are normally of the advertiser, who has the prime responsibility for ensuring that the information given in his advertisements, or, for that matter, in any other sales literature, is correct.

The ultimate sanction

People *are* induced by advertising to part with money in exchange for meaningless 'deeds' of land in Spain which is not the advertiser's to sell. They have been known to post cheques for timeshares in holiday mansions which exist only as a figment in an entrepreneur's imagination. Some will even write out a cheque and put it in the post with a newspaper coupon, in the belief that they are on to a scheme for earning 50 per cent interest per year. There are no limits to the lengths that people can be driven by greed, envy, or simple credulity, and there is no form of legislation that can protect them from the consequences of their own weaknesses. Similarly, no legislation can protect – to take a random sample of human predicaments – women who long for marriage from exploitation by lecherous or scheming males, people with long-standing and incurable medical conditions such as migraine from unscrupulous practitioners, medical or not, who claim to know of a cure, or children from the failure of incompetent teachers to help them achieve their educational potential. A world of total safety is not, at any rate in this life, achievable; though of course that is no reason why we should not still strive for it or something like it.

Nevertheless, it is indisputable that millions of people make purchases each day as a result of advertisements they have heard or seen, and that in the overwhelming majority of instances they are satisfied with the results. For every family that goes on holiday to a hotel advertised as having 'sea views', only to find that the views are on the other side of an airport runway, there are thousands of families who do, in fact, buy holidays as a result of advertisements and who are perfectly happy with the outcome. Our homes are equipped with furniture, our kitchen cupboards stocked with foods, our wardrobes full of clothes that we have seen advertised, have bought, and find no fault with.

Conversely, the public, so often regarded by consumerists, politicians and others as being simple-minded, is quite capable of giving a definitive thumbs-down when the occasion warrants: for example, only one in five of new food products in the UK survives its initial launch. In the end, it is a matter of advertisements making promises about what the advertiser will deliver. The ultimate sanction is the refusal of the consumer to buy, or at any rate to buy a second time. This is why it is in the interests of advertisers and agencies and the media that advertisements should indeed be seen to be legal, decent, honest and truthful.

11 *It may be legal, but is it moral?*

The supply of advertising money (the contemporary equivalent of manna) can only come in the end from us, as workers and buyers, though it is now routed through channels that give control of this social capital to very limited groups.

> Raymond Williams, *Communication 2000*

Advertising is the consequence of a social failure to find means of public information and decision over a wide range of everyday domestic life. This failure . . . is the result of allowing control of the means of production and distribution to pass into minority hands.

> Raymond Williams, *The Listener*, 31 July 1969

The concepts of sexual love, manliness, femininity, maternal feeling are steadily devalued for us by their mercenary association with a brand-name – as though the real human values they represent can be purchased by rushing out and buying a new shaving lotion, a new deodorant, even a new washing-machine.

> Frank Whitehead, *Discrimination and Popular Culture*

In this age of the Ad-man, and of the Ad-man built into our most deeply 'personal' views of happiness and fulfilment, where does 'straight' *communication* end, and consumerist-politico *indoctrination* begin?

> Paul Hoch, *The Newspaper Game*

Much knowledge and many skills must be expertly blended to get the right note of appealing conviction in an advertisement for cat food, or to convey that the girl in the pub with a glass of X's beer is both infectiously gay and thoroughly respectable. But is this the sort of work that an honest man can take pride in?

> The Rev. Edward Rogers, *Expository Times*, November 1965

Large-scale efforts are being made, often with impressive success, to channel our unthinking habits, our purchasing decisions and our thought processes by the use of insights gleaned from psychiatry and the social sciences.

> Vance Packard, *The Hidden Persuaders*

If advertising is to grow up to its power as an instrument of social control, it must develop ideals of social value for the improvement of man, ideas that go beyond keeping him discontented.

Vance Packard, *The Waste Makers*

I have nothing to do with any aspects of advertising; I can't even tell a Cinzano from a Martini. But I trust the public to tell the difference between real life and the ads, which is more than many better-educated worthies seem willing to do.

Edwina Currie, MP, *The Listener*, 5 September 1985

People are not as susceptible to persuasion as the popular literature on the subject would indicate.

Harry Jamieson, *Communication and Persuasion*

The British people are not concerned to limit the freedom of the politician, the journalist and the academic in their choice of the techniques of persuasion they adopt in peddling their ideas and ideals. But when it comes to merchandising goods and property our attitude stiffens. To pull a sharp trick in an election is one thing, to sell shoddy goods under false pretences is another.

Richard Crossman, *New Statesman*, 28 May 1971

It is, in fact, quite difficult for many people to accept that advertisements are, individually, merely attempts by individual firms to sell their goods; that they do this by presenting them in ways which, they hope, will strike a responsive chord with their target audience; and that no ulterior motive is in their minds beyond the profit figure on the bottom line.

Roderick White, *Advertising: What it is and how to do it*

In fairness, it should be noted that advertising does, by stimulating wants, promote a high-output economy, which in turn generates jobs and investment and raises the level of material consumption.

Vance Packard, *The Waste Makers*

It is difficult to know to what extent advertising should take the credit (or the blame) for the vast changes in consumer behaviour which have occurred over the past century or so, since advertising is never the only causal factor at work, and it seems virtually impossible to isolate its influence from that of other social forces.

Vance Packard, *The Hidden Persuaders*

It is by no means difficult to find voices hostile to advertising. They range from the rabid far left, who however are as adept as anyone at the manipulative falsehoods of which they accuse the advertising business, to conservative intellectuals who refuse to acknowledge that they, too, make choices about products and services, and that advertising is one of the sources of information on which those choices are based. In between these poles are the rest of us: those who consider themselves too smart to be 'taken in' and feel secure enough to regard advertising with amused contempt; those who think that TV commercials are an insult to the intelligence (but what about most of the programmes?); those who see ads as a corrupting influence; those who charge advertisers with trivializing the emotions; those who see in advertising an added production cost which is passed on to the consumer; and so on and on. As Roderick White notes in *Advertising: What it is and how to do it*, 'everyone knows all about advertising'.

In defence of itself, the advertising business can point to the jobs created by the stimulation of consumption; to (in Britain) the two television networks and hundreds of newspapers and magazines whose existence is made possible by advertising revenue; to the benefit of advertising to the consumer in indicating what choices are available within a given product range; to the controls, both statutory and voluntary, described in the previous chapter, which protect consumers from advertising excesses; and, *in extremis*, it can be pointed out that advertising people themselves are decent men and women, loving husbands, wives, fathers and mothers, with the same variety of political attitudes and social beliefs and the same sense of responsibility as the rest of us.

There is no resolving the argument, just as there is no chance of changing the vote in a debate about God and Mammon (which some extremists take the argument about advertising to be), Marxism versus capitalism, or today's moral values against yesterday's. However, it is worth looking at the cases for the prosecution and the defence in some detail, if only because it is good to shed light where there is prejudice.

Taste and distaste

First, however, it is necessary to push a certain amount of clutter out of the way. There is an important difference between advertisements which offend against one or other of the Codes of Practice and ones which you or I may not personally like. This is a distinction not always perceived by people who complain about advertisements to the ASA or the IBA. There is a further difference between the fact that you or I personally dislike an advertisement and the assertion that it is therefore immoral, corrupting or in some other way offensive to society at large. This difference is sometimes not perceived by advertising's intellectual critics.

Advertising is highly visible – it would be pointless if it were not – and therefore it inevitably arouses strong reactions. A personality who advertises a particular product on television may well get on one's nerves, especially if one watches a lot of television and sees the commercial repeatedly. Humour, particularly in radio and television commercials, has a way of wearing thin the fourth or fifth time round. This is a problem of which people in the advertising business are well aware, and indeed the IBA's guidelines on radio advertising specifically note that 'undue repetition can rouse irritation and annoyance to listeners and can lose the programme company and the advertiser the good will of potential customers'. But it is the *advertiser's* problem. No harm has been done to the consumer, because he is unlikely to be drawn to buy a product whose advertisements irritate him.

A further problem is posed because we accidentally see, both in the press and on television, many advertisements which are not actually addressed to us. Consequently, drinkers of real ale object to being spoken to as if they were potential customers for gas-pumped lager. Housewives who have better things to do than hold up their children's T-shirts to the light to see if the stains have gone resent the suggestion that this is what they should habitually do in order to ensure that they are using the best detergent for the job. Plenty of people dislike extended discussion of the state of their lavatory pans. But a case cannot be made out of individual prejudices, and advertising is no more invalidated because individual people do not like specific advertisements than is literature because there are some people who find Jane Austen unreadable.

An easy target

Again because it is so visible, advertising is an easy target. Spoof TV commercials are among the items most frequently sent in by amateur scriptwriters to producers of radio and television light entertainment programmes, and there are not many village pantomimes or school concerts which do not include, legitimately enough, easy laughs based on the commercials of the moment.

And surely enough, the image of domestic life reflected in much television advertising is infinitely risible when it is not being curiously – sometimes even endearingly, if one is in the mood – old-fashioned. It posits a nation of housewives (who are, of course, just that – they have no identity beyond their housewifely duties) whose hearts actually do swell with pride when they hold up fresh, soft, whiter-than-white clothes to the light; to whom cleanliness is not merely next to godliness, but indistinguishable from it; who eagerly compare, over a mug of mellow-roasted instant coffee with a neighbour, the merits of this floor cleaner or that washing-up liquid; who see an airing-cupboard piled high with fresh, bouncy 'whites' as the true heart of a good home and a soundly based family life. It would be enough to make one wonder about the home life of people in advertising, were it not for the suspicion that TV commercials of this sort show what upper-middle-class, privately educated twits (of whom, as critics of advertising well know, the staffs of advertising agencies are composed), who have never seen a dirty lavatory or a soiled shirt in their lives, think of us, who have, and of the way we live.

Then again, the ordinary person finds it faintly absurd and perhaps distasteful that Procter & Gamble should spend (in Britain alone) well over £50 million a year to try to persuade people to buy Ariel, Bold, Bounce, Camay, Crest, Daz, Fairy, Flash, Head and Shoulders, Lenor, Pampers and Zest, rather than the virtually indistinguishable products of rival manufacturers. The fact that most of this advertising – over 98 per cent of it on television – is undistinguished and frequently ludicrous does not help to make it acceptable. We may well feel that being shown yet another dumb housewife refusing to hand over her packet of detergent in exchange for two packets of some other brand tests our credulity and tolerance too far. Procter & Gamble's advertisements certainly do little enough to enhance the status of women, or even to acknowledge where it stands today. Many of us may regard a social milieu in which 'I didn't know you had dandruff' (as in a current Head and Shoulders shampoo commercial) is regarded as a reasonable conversational gambit as one which we would prefer not to move in. (Try it at your next party.) Advertising is regrettably often the worst possible advertisement for itself.

Paradoxically, controls, and in particular the IBA Code, have been responsible for some of the features of advertisements which give cause for irritation. The effect of controls has been to make advertisers wary of making product claims or, indeed, of making any positive statements about their wares. There has been a steady retreat into humour and fantasy, genres which, when they flop, flop disastrously. Those who complain that advertisements are divorced from the real world should blame consumerist pressures as much as the advertisers.

The anti-advertising position

So far I have dealt with what might be called popular criticism of advertising, of the kind that might be heard on a bus or in a bar; and certainly it is tedious to try to follow a magazine story through its various 'turns' on the back pages, flanked by serried advertisements, or to be dragged out of an absorbing television play by a 'natural break'. It is time now to address the more fundamental criticisms represented, in the quotations that head this chapter, by Raymond Williams, Frank Whitehead, Paul Hoch and Vance Packard.

A characteristic of these serious critics is that they stand outside the marketplace. Some of them do so literally; it is doubtful, for example, whether Raymond Williams, Fellow of Jesus College, Cambridge, or Frank Whitehead, Reader in English and Education at Sheffield University, are often faced with the dilemma of which detergent to choose from the supermarket shelf, or can have any conception of the complex feelings of a mother of young children trying to tempt their appetites with something novel and attractive. But they and their fellow critics stand outside in a deeper sense. Whitehead, Williams *et al.* are concerned to tell *us*, the poor consumers, what the wicked advertisers, *them*, are doing to *us*, and how simple *we* are to be taken in. There is a strong strain of intellectual snobbery here. The critics are in the same position as librarians who deny children the pleasures of Enid Blyton and Biggles, as schoolteachers who deride their pupils' viewing habits (and then go home to watch *Dallas*), as the self-appointed sages who tell us what kinds of TV programmes we should be given to look at. Ignoring the fact that advertising supports the quality press (as well as the popular), a variety of minority television programmes (as well as *Crossroads* and *The Price Is Right*), and that access to ideas and higher values would be severely damaged if the media supported by advertising were to disappear, they pursue a course of contempt for advertising based, at the left end of the spectrum, on Marxist doctrine or, at the other extreme, on the view that newspapers are for clerks and television is for servants.

Their view of humankind is no less strange than that of the producers of the domestically set commercials referred to earlier. They appear, or affect, to believe that, unless they were there to correct us, a lot of us really could be persuaded that Heineken refreshes the parts other beers cannot reach, or that we really could 'save' money by spending it on cut-price furniture, or that eternal happiness has a price-tag on it, preferably one marked '5p off'. What kind of people do they think we are?

This assumption of superiority is not new, nor is it confined to any one part of the political spectrum. In the 1930s, the Norfolk writer and county lady Lilias Rider Haggard wrote witheringly in her diary (which was published in weekly instalments in a local paper) of the women who were bamboozled by advertisements into buying canned condensed milk for their babies instead of honest cows' milk (such as was produced, for example, on the farms of the Rider Haggard estate). She returned to this topic several times, oblivious to the fact that the reason why Norfolk mothers were buying tinned milk was not that they had been seduced by the tinplate advertisements for Nestlé's which in those days decorated the walls of village shops, but that it was cheaper than fresh milk (and no doubt, given the standards of dairy hygiene at that time, less hazardous to health).

Man has been battered over the centuries by the persuasions of tribal custom, religious proselytization, family pressures and political blackmail – and observe the current ratings of tribalism, religion, the family and politics in public appeal. He is therefore unlikely, having survived all that, to go along unresistingly with the blandishments of a business whose object, according to Aldous Huxley, is to 'find some common desire, some widespread unconscious fear or anxiety, think out some way to relate this wish or fear to the product you have to sell; then, build a bridge of verbal or pictorial symbols over which your customer can pass from fact to compensatory dream, and from the dream to the illusion that your product, when purchased, will make the dream come true'. Huxley was writing in the pre-television age (which makes his suggestions the more absurd, given the seductive potential of, say, the average poster site), but this is a fair summary of one arm of the criticism of advertising. It turns sales chat into something malign – something which, what is more, reaches frighteningly inside us where we cannot see what is going on. Huxley was touching on a myth which, as we shall see later, was to become a rewarding one in the anti-advertising field.

If indeed this psychological power were applied from *one* source with *one* single objective, it would be sinister, as it was in Nazi Germany. But (let us keep hold of reality) we are talking not about advertising, or propaganda, but about *advertisements*. If we are being sold dreams and illusions (as of course we are also when we see a play or a film, read a novel or a poem, listen to music, look at a painting), they are self-cancelling. Dreams of being able to talk posh like Ian Carmichael if we buy a certain brand of Californian wine conflict with dreams of being accepted as good neighbours if we wash our kitchen floors with Flash; dreams of wiping twenty years off our faces by washing them with Camay fight with dreams of holding our heads up in the street by refusing to buy stores' own brand instant coffee and of attracting grand friends by handing round a packet of chocolate mints. There is no more room for all these dreams than there is for the kind that politicians (or academics, for that matter) peddle to us. As a result, we confine our dreaming to a few private ambitions, recognizing advertisement-bound dreams for what they are.

Packard and after

Vance Packard's *The Hidden Persuaders* was the first popular book to warn the consumer against the wiles of advertisers. Writers like Orwell and Huxley had agonized intellectually about advertising, but Packard was a pioneer in quoting chapter and verse on the mal-practices of named advertisers. *The Hidden Persuaders* is still widely used as a text at the bottom end of the anti-advertising mar-ket, that is to say by teachers of 'media studies' and similar courses in secondary schools, for all that it first appeared in Britain in 1960 and was based largely on examples of American advertising practice during the 1950s and earlier. This was a period when television advertising was still in its infancy and exploring the boundaries of its own world. Many of the practices deplored by Packard have since been outlawed in the United States, and either have never been employed in Britain or have been outlawed either voluntarily or by statute. In spite of recent revisions, Packard's is substantially a his-tory book.

But the tale he had to tell was indeed a frightening one. One aspect of it that took a particular hold on Britain was the matter of sublim-inal advertising – the flashing on to the TV screen of messages so brief that the conscious mind does not take them in, but which pass straight to the subconscious. When Packard's book was published, TV advertising was very much a novelty in Britain, and people – abetted by the press, which had lost a great deal of revenue with the introduction of commercial television – were prepared to believe almost anything of it. Subliminal techniques reminded them of Orwell's *1984*. The Korean War, with its accusations and counter-accusations of 'brain-washing', was not far behind. At a more popu-lar level, television was still regarded with awe; that you could enjoy the show at the London Palladium without leaving your armchair in, say, Macclesfield seemed like a kind of contemporary magic. What could be more likely than that some sinister *they* were taking advantage of this only half-understood medium to seduce the inno-cent viewer and steal the very cash from his pocket? No one thought to ask by what mechanism a subliminal sales message, planted in the subconscious, could be made to surface at a relevant moment, in a shop, instead of at one (perhaps in the bath or in bed) when it would be commercially wasted.

Nevertheless, *The Hidden Persuaders* was influential. It was one of the inputs which created the consumerist movement and ultimately, in Britain, the Consumers' Association. The setting-up of the British Code of Advertising Practice in 1961, one year after Packard's book appeared here, was no accident. British society was in a mood to look askance at advertising; and politicians, among others, identified it as a populist yet politically safe cause with vote-catching appeal. It was no surprise when, in 1963, the Pilkington Report on Broadcasting came out with a distinct anti-advertising bias. News of an easy target spreads fast.

'It costs to advertise'

A persistent obsession with critics of advertising is that heavily advertised products cost substantially more than those which merely sidle shyly on to the retail shelves. Indeed, they may; but one does not necessarily follow from the other.

The cost of advertising to the consumer is an argument carefully nurtured by those who sell unbranded and unadvertised goods; 'You'd be surprised if I told you who made this, but naturally I can't divulge a trade secret. The reason why it's so cheap, you can see, is that he doesn't advertise this one . . .' The huge growth in recent years of stores' 'own brand' products is a testimony to the belief that the difference in price between these and branded goods represents advertising costs. In fact, as anyone who knows anything about the pricing of products for the marketplace will confirm, although whether or not a product is heavily advertised may have a bearing on the manufacturer's recommended price, the difference is not directly related to the cost of advertising.

Since the abolition of Retail Price Maintenance, products have tended to be priced at what the market will pay. Thus, customers in village shops will pay a few pence extra for most ordinary everyday goods, acknowledging that this is the price of not having to make a journey to the nearest town for, say, a bottle of washing-up detergent; thus, also, there are customers who will buy a brand to which they are loyal, or to which they have been converted by advertising, even if it is a few pence dearer. The difference in price is a measurement, not of the cost of advertising, but of the customer's financial ability to make a choice. A moment's thought will show that although £50 million a year sounds a lot for Procter & Gamble's advertising budget, it represents an insignificant amount of money per pack when spread over the millions of boxes of detergent, tubes of toothpaste and bottles of shampoo sold each year; and that insignificant amount is easily recovered through the economies of scale achieved by increased demand stimulated by advertising.

It can be argued that customers should not have to pay for buying a brand name – but then in the reality of the marketplace they can choose not to. What their extra coppers pay for if they choose a branded product is open to question; but it is not, in most cases, the cost of advertising. As Harry Henry, former Visiting Professor of Marketing Communications at Cranfield, wrote in 1964: 'The trouble with so many critics of advertising is that they have never had the opportunity of sitting in on the decision-making process when pricing policy is under review, and thus have not the faintest conception of the exhaustive consideration given to the various elements of cost . . . and how these are weighed against the desirability of coming up with a final selling price which, while being as low as possible, still gives sufficient elbow-room for the market potential to be properly developed.' He was writing about a trading climate in which, with Retail Price Maintenance still in force, pricing at source was more significant than it is today, but his basic message still holds good.

Advertising and market power

It is necessary now to examine the argument that the command of the marketplace taken by those companies able to afford large advertising budgets leads to the concentration of power into too few hands, and that that power is then used to the disadvantage of the consumer. The fact that in 1983, for example, about 10 per cent of Britain's total advertising spend came from the ten top-spending companies might appear to support this view. But this advertising concerned over 60 different products or services, a number which is greatly increased if the individual brands of cigarettes, cigars and tobaccos are taken into account. Three of the 'top ten', Mars,

Rowntree Mackintosh and Cadbury Schweppes, were competing in the same market, and a cursory glance at the shelves of any sweet-shop will show that, while these companies' products are prominent, they have to fight competitors both great and small. None of the three is in anything like a commanding position in the market, which is itself, of course, only part of a larger market for snacks, 'treats' and children's pocket-money. Surely you would have to be politically rabid to see in Mars Ltd a potentially evil power.

There are other objections that can be made to the three leading companies' expenditure (some £84 million in 1983) on confectionery advertising, in particular that it was spent in disregard of the effects of chocolate on children's teeth. Campaigners *against* sugar, tobacco, alcoholic drink and meat, and *for* fibre, animal liberation, vegetarianism and the good, honest English apple all put advertising high in their demonology. But if advertising is to take the blame for the state of our teeth, it must also be given the credit for, for example, the cleaner state of our homes, clothes and persons than, say, a couple of generations ago; that more people are aware that there are alternatives for savings and insurance to the so-called 'industrial' insurance companies with their relatively poor returns; that issues like the domestically important one of the relative costs of heating by different energy sources are continually exposed and discussed in advertisements; that the market is an open place where values and prices can be readily assessed.

What, then, about the further charge against advertising, that it has too much power over the media in terms both of their content and of its tendency to concentrate ownership into too few hands? It is true that if an advertiser withdrew from a newspaper or a television station because of an editorial item we should probably never know about it; but what we do know is that many newspapers, periodicals and television programmes frequently carry editorial material which runs counter to the interests of substantial advertisers. Journalists and television programme staff are powerful enough to ensure that editorial and advertising are kept apart, not only physically but also in policy terms, and the consumer movement, for all its identification of the media as enemies, would not exist if it were not for the willingness of the media to give extensive coverage to its affairs and concerns. (Incidentally, it may be worth noting here that, perhaps on the principle that the devil should not have all the best tunes, the Consumers' Association has become one of the most persistent direct mailers in Britain, using techniques closely modelled on those of other prominent organizations in this field such as Reader's Digest and the Automobile Association.) The controls that critics of the media should be worrying more about are those imposed by the law of libel (which in Britain prevents the exposure of much public and commercial corruption), official devices such as the Official Secrets Act, the D-notice system and the 30-year rule on public records, and by the clubroom conspiracies that keep hidden 'inconvenient' information.

The collapse of the *News Chronicle* in 1960 despite a circulation of over one million is often quoted as an example of the power of advertising over the media, and of what Raymond Williams calls the 'open definition of the success or failure of a newspaper in terms of the condition required by its advertisers: the reliable delivery of an effective body of purchasers'. But as almost everyone knows who has heard Fleet Street mentioned – leave alone those who know anything about its history – what has led until recently to the closure of newspapers is not the malign influence of the advertising business but the fact that managements and workforces have clung to methods of printing with which Caxton could soon have familiarized himself. Computer-based film typesetting and web-offset printing, the so-called 'modern' technology, have been in use by provincial newspaper printers for 20 years. They fractionalize the number of people required to produce newspapers, as Rupert Murdoch and Robert Maxwell are showing. Rid of the burden of overmanning and outdated working practices, the *News Chronicle* would today make a healthy profit with its million copies a day. At a more local and specialized level, cheap printing has put publication within reach of virtually any group of people with something to say, whether or not they can attract advertisers. Technical limitations have so far prevented a similar growth in access to television, though Channel Four has expanded the range of viewpoints and topics now reaching the screen in Britain. There is little doubt that eventually television will follow radio in embracing a wider range of media ownership, subject only to Parliament's willingness to set the monster free.

The huckster's spiel

Advertising people find themselves in some difficulty when they come to defend themselves against their critics. They are, in a real sense, the legatees of the huckster tradition, and this becomes quite clear when they are heard talking about their work. Unfortunately, the language of the market-stall does not necessarily go with the image of social and commercial probity that the advertising business as a whole yearns to display.

When an advertising man writes a book and entitles it *Don't Tell My Mother I'm in Advertising – She Thinks I'm a Pianist in a Brothel*; when another describes his job as 'the most fun you can have with your clothes on'; when we read in *Campaign* the shrill phrase-smithing which is advertising people's customary style of communication; when the marketing manager of a famous company is heard to say that 'if my mum sat in on a research debrief listening to us talking about deep psychological motivation, she would think we were all off our heads'; we can only conclude that advertising people should set about trying to make friends. But the reason for the continual personal hype, the quest for attention ('Look, no guns!' was an advertising man's opening gambit in an interview with me, as he threw back his jacket in a theatrical gesture), the reliance on the support of 'systems' which sound to most of us little better than charlatanry, is that advertising as a business and advertising people as people are desperately insecure. This is true both in the personal sense – hiring and firing is all in a day's work, and an agency can go up like a rocket or down like a stick at the speed of light – and because of the lack of certainties in the business as a whole.

One of the oldest jokes in advertising is about the advertiser who said: 'Of course advertising pays – half the time. The trouble is, I don't know which half.' The experience of Procter & Gamble with a low suds detergent for front-loading washing machines which they originally called Cheer illustrates the truth behind the joke. Cheer was launched in a test market in 1962. It flopped. Since the platform for detergents had traditionally been their lathering properties, perhaps it was not surprising that a product whose low-lathering characteristic was the main selling proposition would have a rough time in the marketplace. At the time, front-loading washing machines were still novel; housewives in Britain had been sold, and remained faithful to, the top-loader, in which a plenitude of suds testified to the thoroughness of the wash. Cheer disappeared from the shelves, to be relaunched three years later as Bold. This time it took off, to such an extent that Lever, feeling threatened, felt bound to counter with a low suds detergent called Skip. Skip limped its way into obscurity; but its descendant, Persil Automatic, skipped its way into the market leadership league.

There is no explaining why something called Cheer should fail and the same product, renamed Bold, should succeed. Even Vance Packard admitted, in *The Hidden Persuaders*, that 'it is difficult to know to what extent advertising should take the credit (or the blame) for the vast changes in consumer behaviour which have occurred over the past century or so'. The advertising world is one of uncertainties, which is why it feels bound to create certainties of its own; hence the confident talk and the hyperboles. Advertising people tend to want to forget such shameful episodes as the Strand cigarette campaign of the late 1950s (when cigarette advertisements were still permitted on British television) which majored on the phrase that 'You're never alone with a Strand', supported by a Sinatra-like figure being just that, but did not realize that lighting a cigarette to make it look as if you had something to do was the hallmark of the social reject.

When advertising contains the seeds of its own destruction, the seeds grow; Strand cigarettes were never seen again. The dream that Strand advertising peddled was evidently not an attractive one. The consumer, in the end, calls the tune. And for all the confident tones in which market research announces its findings (and such findings no doubt justified the launch of Cheer and Skip), it remains true that no one in advertising actually *knows* what can be sold or to whom. Advertising's critics believe that they know. They are the dealers in certainties. Advertising's practitioners know better. It is perhaps to be regretted that they are driven so often to sound as if they know all the answers – but then they have to earn a living. Inside advertising, a considerable amount of time away from the copywriting pad and the drawing-board is spent in questioning the assumptions that underlie the whole business; and the fact that that is so is society's protection against the nightmares that disturb the sleep of advertising's critics.

12 Advertising as a career

Fast-moving, glamorous, exciting, well-paid: these are typical words that spring to many people's minds when they think of advertising, and they are magnetic words for many thinking of a future career.

As with most generalizations, the words represent a half-truth. Advertising consists, as was noted earlier in this book, of far more than the agencies, which are its most visible aspect and most nearly deserve such a testimonial. But even in the agencies there is much mundane work to be done. Advertising can be fast-moving, but the complex processes of creating, placing and producing advertisements also involves, as we have pointed out, meticulous planning and checking, accounting and budgeting. Advertising has its glamorous side – but behind this public face there are many people doing not particularly glamorous jobs in far from glamorous offices. Like any creative job, advertising has its exciting moments – but they are the peaks in a working life that also contains many troughs. As for pay, there is something like a star system comparable to that of the stage (and just as uncertain). It is true that the creative head of a large London agency will (in 1986) earn round about £40000, with a benefits package made up of a prestige company car, health insurance, pension and so on worth about the same amount again, while some top-rankers are on £100000 or more; but most people in the business can expect to be paid at about the same rate as they would receive for equivalent jobs elsewhere.

Nevertheless, advertising continues to be one of the most sought-after careers. In 1983, a typical year, one London agency had 2000 applications for four jobs for graduate trainees. Another, with six jobs going, attracted 1300 applicants. All told, the 270-odd agencies take in 80 to 120 new graduates each year, who will start (in 1986) on £7000–£8000 in London and rather less, occasionally much less, in the provinces. Graduates are not, of course, the only intake. Even a clerical or secretarial vacancy for a junior can attract up to 250 applications.

The agencies are the most visible face of advertising, and the natural first choice of someone planning a career. But, as anyone who has read this book will know, advertising has other aspects and other potential employers. It is worth remembering, too, that about one-quarter of agency jobs are outside London.

Of the many who apply, few are chosen. Most hopefuls have not the ghost of a chance of landing a job, and indeed many are not serious applicants in the sense that they *particularly* want a career in advertising. It is easy to weed out those for whom it is just one option among many, and there are so many genuine applicants that no one has time to waste on faint-hearts. The agency mentioned earlier, which received 1300 applications, rejected 94 per cent of them on the strength of a cursory skim over the application forms.

Having said all that, it must be added that advertising is always in the market for new people. It uses up talent at an alarming rate and, depending as it does on young ideas, it needs a steady flow of people coming in at the bottom. Advertising folk like to say that theirs is a 'people business'; it may seem strange, in view of that, that recruitment procedures are apparently so ramshackle. This is probably due to the fact that there are no recognized entry qualifications, and it is impossible to say who will succeed in a world where commercial nous, instinct and inspiration – qualities which must be tested mainly on the shop floor – are needed in a roughly equal balance.

The advertising world

The agencies apart, jobs wholly or partly involved with advertising are to be found in the following areas:

Advertisers often have their own advertising staff, who may be part of the marketing or publicity departments. The work here could include the production of sales brochures, promotional material and instruction handbooks, as well as mainstream advertising. Exhibition work, the organization of in-store promotions and merchandising, public relations, press liaison and sponsorship are other likely duties. Mail order and catalogue companies and large retailers are among possible employers. There is a fair amount of movement from advertisers to agencies, and a few years' experience with a client company is a good base for someone who wants to move on. A typical starting post might be as a marketing or publicity assistant, leading to promotion through the marketing side or a sideways step into brand management. Alternatively, in-store merchandising or exhibition work has the merit of providing contact with the market-place – highly valuable experience in the consumer field.

The media employ large numbers of people to service their advertising departments. Telephone space-selling, though limited in prospects and unlikely therefore to be a long-term career choice (though there are opportunities in larger media groups for those with training expertise), is by no means to be despised as a way of getting to know about advertising from the media end. There is also busy traffic work in a media sales department, ensuring that advertisements are proofed and checked and that deadlines are met. In radio and television, the sales staff check and assemble the commercials ready for broadcasting. Television and the larger press companies maintain research and information staffs whose job is to provide advertisers with up-to-date information on, for example, audiences or readerships and their characteristics. Some companies provide marketing services for advertisers. Television companies have sales staff in London and major provincial centres as well as at their own regional headquarters.

Service companies, often quite small, offer another possible starting-point for entrants with specific skills such as an art or design background and ability. Advertising depends very heavily on outside design, research, production and finishing facilities, but because many of these units are small they can only take people who can make a useful contribution from day one. But a small studio would be a useful place, say, for someone with an art or design diploma, plus of course creative flair, to start. An interesting and varied portfolio would count for more than a handsomely produced c.v. There are also some opportunities in production departments for people with a background in printing, especially if they have good experience of a range of printing processes.

Are you right for the job?

It cannot be emphasized too strongly that advertising is both highly competitive and highly critical of performance. It is no place for people who want to coast along, doing no more than they are asked to do. It is a hard, not particularly sympathetic world dominated by commercial reality mixed with built-in insecurity. There are no soft options or cosy niches, and there is no room for passengers. Advertising provides a working environment to which, quite simply, some people are unsuited.

Although advertising people are often thought of, with some justification, as cynical, they take their own business very seriously indeed and require a similar degree of commitment from newcomers. It should go without saying that no one should seek a career in advertising unless he accepts the underlying commercial philosophy and is prepared, if necessary, to defend it.

The range of jobs available in advertising is wide, as has already been indicated, and working conditions vary enormously; but there are certain characteristics common to most of them, imposed by the nature of the business itself. Here is a check-list of some of the *qualities*, as distinct from *qualifications*, that newcomers need:

* *Adaptability*. Few people in advertising are able to concentrate on just one piece of work at a time. They tend to be working on a number of different things which are at various stages of development or progress, and some of this work will never reach the final stages for one reason or another. They need to be able to juggle with priorities, 'drop everything' if necessary to deal with a sudden crisis, and keep tabs on a variety of items.

* *Staying-power*. In a world of deadlines, heavy traffic and sometimes highly strung personalities (though it should always be *the other person* who gives way to tension), considerable stamina is needed – both mental and

physical – if the job is to be enjoyed rather than endured. Patience is a considerable virtue, and a short fuse a distinct disadvantage.

* *Commitment*. If you like to get home at the same time every night, expect to have every evening free, and regard your weekends as sacrosanct, you are unlikely to be happy in advertising. You must be prepared to burn the midnight oil, work through the weekend if necessary, take work home or make sudden trips away. In many advertising jobs there is a certain amount of socializing – with bosses, colleagues, clients, suppliers – which is reckoned to oil the wheels and is more or less obligatory.

* *Getting on with people*. Advertising is not a business where there is much pulling of rank, but you must be able to get on with people higher and lower than you in the hierarchies of client companies as well as those in your own organization. In almost any branch of advertising, you will find yourself at one time or another acting as your employer's ambassador, and you must be able to cope with that. The ability to get good work and service out of service departments in the organization and suppliers outside is an important skill.

* *Mobility*. The mobility of advertising people is well known. Someone who hopes for a secure career with one employer, and who worries overmuch about pension rights, is unlikely to be happy. At the same time, loyalty is required. It is also wise, because advertising people are often sought after as teams; and if you gather round you trusted and like-minded colleagues, you are often more marketable as a group than individually. What is more, if a colleague you know and like moves on, he is quite likely to ask you to follow him.

* *Literacy and numeracy*. Most advertising jobs demand more than average ability to present and absorb written information, which has nothing to do with O-level results. A readable essay and a well-worked-out marketing strat-

egy are two entirely different things. Numeracy is also highly prized and is specifically mentioned by many recruiters as an increasingly important requirement in such fast-moving, quick-thinking situations as negotiations over media rates and budgets.

* *Confidentiality*. Much work in advertising is confidential and that confidentiality must be honoured. Someone working on an account in an agency, or selling media space or time, or preparing advertisements for a future campaign, is in possession of commercial information which is potentially valuable to a competitor. This applies equally to any incidental information about clients or associates which is acquired in the course of work.

The way in

Advertising is traditionally an open-minded business which regards ability to do the job as more important than paper qualifications. There is at least one agency head who began his career (in a different agency) as a messenger-boy, and there are many highly placed people who came into advertising at secretarial or clerical level – though it must be admitted that, with increasing emphasis on graduate recruitment, such rags-to-riches stories are likely to be rarer in future. Nevertheless, if you take a random sample of people who have made advertising their career and achieved success, they tend to reveal a wide spectrum of backgrounds and entry points, confirming that the business is still more open than most.

It is particularly notable in offering genuine equal opportunities to women, and this was true long before equal opportunities legislation was even thought of. Almost one in four agency executives are women, and in some areas – particularly media planning and buying, market research and audio-visual production – the proportion of women employed approaches or reaches half. Secretarial entry is not necessarily a dead end, and indeed can provide a sound base on which a career can be built. Away from the agencies, women are

equally prominent in advertisers' marketing and publicity departments and in media sales and marketing.

Jobs for beginners tend not to be advertised, and for most newcomers it is largely a matter of searching for opportunities. There are
three main categories of entrants:

School-leavers.   The ebb and flow of traffic in all areas of the business provides employment opportunities for school- and college-
leavers with secretarial skills, numeracy, an eye for detail and sound
certificate results. Employers look for a positive interest in advertising and some appreciation of how the kind of job aimed for fits into
the general scheme of things.

Graduate entry.   This, as has already been indicated, is the major
source of new recruits to advertising. There is no 'milk round' as
such, but the larger agencies maintain contacts with university and
polytechnic careers officers. Large numbers of graduates write round
'on spec', and if they have something out of the ordinary to offer,
and can present it well in their letters, they are likely to get at least
some interviews.

Advertising people are searching interviewers – as they can afford
to be, given the proportion of applicants to vacancies. Some of the
larger London agencies have highly structured procedures involving, for example, mock business situations. Others invite comment
on a selection of advertisements. Elsewhere, interviews are along
more conventional lines. From time to time, advertising indulges in
bursts of self-criticism over its haphazard recruitment procedures.
'The quality of many agency selection procedures and training programmes,' wrote the managing director of one leading London
agency in 1985, 'remains appallingly low. This manifests itself at its
simplest level in the inability of some agencies to even reply to
applications promptly, if at all. Not a good introduction for someone
interested in getting into the communications industry.' Others
would argue that advertising is a highly individual business not
amenable to fixed procedures, which might in any case favour more
middle-of-the-road candidates and overlook the potential high-
flyers.

Graduate entrants are accepted from all disciplines, but in advertisers' marketing departments people with a business-related degree may have a slight edge. In the relevant areas, art degrees or diplomas are welcome, but the work in the applicant's portfolio is more important.

Mature entrants. A small but significant number of people move into advertising as a second career, but it is not an opportunity for someone who has simply become bored with his present job. To overcome the problem that they are late starters, mature applicants need to have something extra to offer. In many cases, this will be experience in a specialized field; for example, from time to time there are vacancies for experienced pharmacists as copywriters for pharmaceutical manufacturers, while agencies with substantial food accounts occasionally take on experienced home economists. One experienced teacher found a job writing educational materials for a pet food company. Such jobs are among the few that are normally advertised, usually in the trade press of the specialism concerned. But relevant specialist experience is not enough on its own. Candidates will also be expected to show the qualities of resilience, commitment and initiative that would be asked of entrants to advertising at any level.

Starting off

It seems to be generally agreed that, mature entrants apart, an 'on spec' application is just as likely to succeed as any other. Obviously some casual applications will go unanswered, and others will produce only a formal rejection, but many persistent applicants with the ability to sell themselves effectively in a letter do get interviewed, and some get appointed. Gimmickry can sometimes work – though, when it flops, it often flops badly. An applicant who turned up at a major agency dressed in a gorilla suit badly misjudged the situation and was shown the door; but one designer got his first job by sending round his application packaged like a bottle of whisky.

New recruits into any branch of the advertising business can expect to spend their first weeks or months doing dogsbody jobs ranging from keeping the studio tidy to messenger work. In the larger agencies where functions are departmentalized, recruits are likely to spend a period in account management or planning, where they will gradually be given small, and eventually larger, areas of responsibility. In smaller agencies, the work may well be more varied and there will be greater pressure to make a positive contribution early on. There is a large measure of on-the-job training, partly because each office tends to develop its own style of organization and working procedures, depending on the mixture of skills available. Beyond this, part-time courses are available through advertising's own training body, the CAM (Communications, Advertising and Marketing) Foundation. One- or two-year courses lead to the Certificate in Communication Studies, which covers such related topics as marketing and public relations, as well as advertising. Holders of the Certificate may study for a further year to obtain the CAM Diploma. This involves specializing in three (five for an Honours Diploma) out of ten available areas of study. Candidates for CAM qualifications must have at least five certificate passes, including English Language, or equivalent educational achievements. Certain business and marketing qualifications exempt Diploma candidates from having first gained the CAM Certificate.

Advertising is an exceptionally volatile business; and even without making a positive move, people can find themselves with new employers as a result of partnership splits, takeovers and amalgamations. But the ambitious advertising person will, after a few years' groundwork (preferably in a variety of departments), start to make or look for his own opportunities. It is wise to aim for breadth of experience, even within the same field. In media sales, for example, spells in research and information help to fill out the experience of field selling. In an advertiser's office, experience of dealing with agents and the wholesale trade complements work directed at consumer level. The relevant professional journals (see below) are a good source of information about second and third jobs – not only in their advertisements but also in the news snippets they carry about people who are moving on.

There is a considerable drop-out rate among advertising people in their thirties; and if you cherish long-term security to any great extent, then advertising is probably not for you. It is generally agreed that survivors need to be well up the career ladder – at account director level in an agency, for example, or marketing manager for a client company – by their mid-thirties. And beyond that? Here are some sobering words from an agency creative head: 'It's a dangerous business, for God's sake. As you start pushing forty you figure you have maybe ten years left. No one really knows what happens because agencies are comparatively young.'

In a world of their own

Advertising is a highly introspective business whose practitioners to a large extent live in each other's pockets. You can get the feel of this by dropping in round about lunchtime at any pub near an agency. Anyone planning to work in advertising will be expected to play a full part in the game in which advertising is seen as the centre of the business universe. A candidate interviewed for an agency job must learn something about the agency's recent history, its present client list and recent acquisitions, and current campaigns. Information like this is picked up easily enough by a thorough weekly reading, over a period, of the advertising trade paper *Campaign. Marketing Week, Media Week* and *Broadcast* are the equivalent journals in other related business sectors. Outside the centres of large cities, they normally have to be ordered. Similarly, an applicant to a television programme company, or to magazine or newspaper publishers, should do some homework on the medium concerned: its market, its special areas of interest, and so on. Advertisers will expect applicants to have acquired some detailed knowledge of their products, markets, advertising and commercial background.

Because it is to some extent an enclosed world, advertising offers most of its best opportunities to those who are already on the inside. This works in favour of those people who are interested and determined enough to take an initial job at whatever level is offered.

Organizations and addresses

The Advertising Association, Abford House, 15 Wilton Road, London SW1V 1NJ. The umbrella organization which covers the interests of all sectors of the advertising business. Publications include a series of 'Student's Briefs', for school and college use, on various aspects of broadcasting, and a careers guide.

The Advertising Standards Authority, Brook House, Torrington Place, London WC1E 7HN. Supervises the observation of the British Code of Advertising Practice and the British Code of Sales Promotion Practice, copies of which are available free of charge. Monitors certain categories of advertising on a regular basis. Responds to complaints from the public about any advertising *except* that on radio or television, and publishes a monthly *Case Report* on its findings.

Association of Independent Radio Contractors, Regina House, 259–269 Old Marylebone Road, London NW1 5RA. The trade organization of the Independent Local Radio Companies.

British Direct Marketing Association, 1 New Oxford Street, London WC1A 1NQ. The trade organization for direct mail and direct response users. Supervises the observation by members of the Direct Marketing Code of Practice and supports the Mailing Preference Service (see below).

The CAM Foundation, Abford House, 15 Wilton Road, London SW1V 1NJ. The education and training body for those in communications, advertising and marketing. Organizes the Certificate in Communication Studies and CAM Diploma courses and examinations, and provides seminars and discussions for senior people in the communications business.

Incorporated Society of British Advertisers, 44 Hertford Street, London W1Y 8AE. Represents the interests of advertisers and advises on contractual, legislative and other matters in relation to their involvement in advertising.

Independent Broadcasting Authority, 70 Brompton Road, London SW3 1EY. Publishes the IBA Code of Advertising Standards and Practice (copy free on request) and more detailed guidelines for radio and television programme companies. Receives and considers complaints from the public about broadcast advertising on ITV, Channel Four and Independent Local Radio stations, and publishes a monthly summary of its findings.

Independent Television Companies Association, Knighton House, 56 Mortimer Street, London W1N 8AN. The trade association of the ITV companies. Offers guidance to advertisers and agencies on advertising matters. Clears scripts and finished commercials. Publications include ten booklets, Notes of Guidance, on various aspects of television advertising, and also a file on Careers in Independent Television, for which a charge is made. Inquiries on the careers guide to the Training Adviser.

Institute of Practitioners in Advertising, 44 Belgrave Square, London SW1X 8QS. The industry body and professional institute for UK advertising agencies. IPA members handle about 90 per cent of advertising placed by UK agencies. Provides legal and marketing advice to members, education and training facilities for both trainees and senior personnel, and general support services.

Mailing Preference Service, Freepost 22, London W1E 7EZ. Enables members of the public to have their names removed from the mailing lists of over 100 leading direct mail originators, or alternatively to have their names added so that they receive direct mail in certain categories of products or services.

Newspaper Publishers Association, 6 Bouverie Street, London EC4Y 8AY.   The organization of national daily and Sunday newspapers (though not all of them belong). Provides a protection service for readers whose response to mail order advertisements results in unsatisfactory treatment.

The Newspaper Society, Whitefriars House, 6 Carmelite Street, London EC4Y 0BL.   The organization of provincial daily and weekly papers. Provides a protection service for readers of these papers similar to that of the NPA.

Outdoor Advertising Association, 3 Dean Farrar Street, London SW1 9LG.   The trade association of outdoor advertising contractors.

Periodical Publishers Association, Imperial House, Kingsway, London WC2.   The organization of magazine and periodical publishers. Provides a protection service for readers similar to that of the NPA and Newspaper Society.

Select bibliography

This is only a beginners' list of books on advertising from which I have omitted practical handbooks. The titles listed below explore in greater depth some of the more general themes touched on in this book.

Barnes, Michael (ed.): *The Three Faces of Advertising*, The Advertising Association, 1975. Sixteen contributions on the ethics, economics and effects of advertising, representing a broad spectrum of opinion drawn from within and outside the advertising business.

Douglas, Torin: *The Complete Guide to Advertising*, Macmillan, 1984. An ambitious title. The book does not quite live up to it, but it contains a selection of campaign case-histories and its great merit is the wealth of examples of TV stills, press ads and posters reproduced in full colour. There is a helpful section on printing processes.

Packard, Vance: *The Hidden Persuaders*, Penguin, 1960, and revisions. As noted in Chapter 11, this is now to some extent a history text, but it has been an influential book and has a place in the background to the consumer movement.

Tunstall, Jeremy: *The Media in Britain*, Constable, 1983. Concerned mainly with the editorial content of the media, but relevant on media groupings, the relationship between advertising and content, and recent changes in advertising support for the media.

Turner, E. S.: *The Shocking History of Advertising*, Penguin, 1965. A light-hearted romp through some of the grislier moments in the early history of the advertising business. However, present-day Codes of Conduct owe something to the need to outlaw some of the practices described by Turner.

White, Roderick: *Advertising – What it is and how to do it*, McGraw-Hill, 1980. An insider's view of the business. Some of the detailed information is already out of date, and Roderick White's style is a little too jokey at times, but there is a great deal of useful detail and a particularly valuable chapter on advertising in foreign markets.

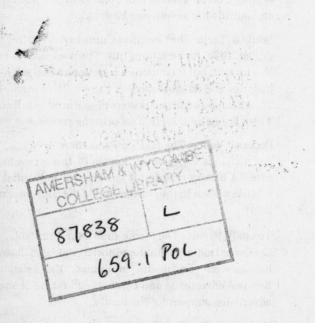